MARITAL AND FAMILY COUNSELING

Publication No. 941
AMERICAN LECTURE SERIES®

A Publication in
The BANNERSTONE DIVISION of AMERICAN LECTURES
IN SOCIAL AND REHABILITATION PSYCHOLOGY

Editors of the Series

JOHN G. CULL, Ph.D.
Director, Regional Counselor Training Program
Department of Rehabilitation Counseling
Virginia Commonwealth University
Fishersville, Virginia

RICHARD E. HARDY, Ed.D.
Diplomate in Counseling Psychology
Chairman, Department of Rehabilitation Counseling
Virginia Commonwealth University
Richmond, Virginia

The American Lecture Series in Social and Rehabilitation Psychology offers books which are concerned with man's role in his milieu. Emphasis is placed on how this role can be made more effective in a time of social conflict and a deteriorating physical environment. The books are oriented toward descriptions of what future roles should be and are not concerned exclusively with the delineation and definition of contemporary behavior. Contributors are concerned to a considerable extent with prediction through the use of a functional view of man as opposed to a descriptive, anatomical point of view.

Books in this series are written mainly for the professional practitioner; however, academicians will find them of considerable value in both under-graduate and graduate courses in the helping services.

Techniques and
Approaches in
MARITAL AND
FAMILY COUNSELING

RICHARD E. HARDY

JOHN G. CULL

CHARLES C THOMAS • PUBLISHER
Springfield • *Illinois* • *U.S.A.*

Published and Distributed Throughout the World by
CHARLES C THOMAS • PUBLISHER
Bannerstone House
301–327 East Lawrence Avenue, Springfield, Illinois, U.S.A.

© *1974, by* CHARLES C THOMAS • PUBLISHER
ISBN 0-398-03093-6
Library of Congress Catalog Card Number: 73-20423

With THOMAS BOOKS careful attention is given to all details of
manufacturing and design. It is the Publisher's desire to present books that
are satisfactory as to their physical qualities and artistic possibilities and
appropriate for their particular use. THOMAS BOOKS will be true to
those laws of quality that assure a good name and good will.

Printed in the United States of America
CC-11

Library of Congress Cataloging in Publication Data

Hardy, Richard E
  Techniques and approaches in marital and family counseling.

  (American lecture series, publication no. 941. A publication in the
Bannerstone division of American lectures in social and rehabilitation
psychology)
  1. Marriage counseling—Addresses, essays, lectures. 2. Psychotherapy—
Addresses, essays, lectures. I. Cull, John G., joint author. II. Title. III.
Title: Martial and family counseling.
HQ10.H28   362.8'2   73-20423   ISBN 0-398-03093-6

CONTRIBUTORS

JAMES F. ALEXANDER, Ph.D.: Associate professor at the University of Utah. He is also currently coordinator of community practicum training, and consultant to various agencies (Salt Lake Veterans Administration Hospital, Utah State Juvenile Court, and Salt Lake Comprehensive Community Mental Health Center). He has authored numerous journal articles and convention papers on family interaction and family therapy including *Journal of Consulting and Clinical Psychology* and *Journal of Marriage and the Family.*

CHARLES ANSELL, Ed.D.: Dr. Ansell received his Doctorate at Teachers College, Columbia University. Additionally he received psychoanalytic training from the National Psychological Association for Psychoanalysis where he studied under Theodore Reik. Dr. Ansell, a qualified analyst, has been in continuous private practice as a psychologist and marriage and family counselor in Sherman Oaks, California since 1960. He is past president of the Los Angeles County Psychological Association; editor of the California State Psychological Association Newsletter; and President of the California State Psychological Association; a frequent lecturer in special programs at UCLA, State colleges and psychiatric hospital staffs, and is consultant to various institutions and social agencies.

JOSEPH CASSIUS, Ph.D.: Dr. Cassius received his Doctorate in Clinical Psychology from Yeshiva University in New York. He has been trained in Transactional Analysis, Gestalt Therapy and Neo-Reichian Analytic Therapy. He specializes in protracted group and family treatment.

JOHN G. CULL, Ph.D.: Professor and Director, Regional Counselor Training Program, Department of Rehabilitation Counseling, Virginia Commonwealth University, Fishersville, Virginia; Adjunct Professor of Psychology and Education, School of General Studies, University of Virginia, Charlottesville, Virginia;

Technical Consultant, Rehabilitation Services Administration, United States Department of Health, Education and Welfare, Washington, D.C.; Editor, American Lecture Series in Social and Rehabilitation Psychology, Charles C Thomas, Publisher; Lecturer Medical Department, Woodrow Wilson Rehabilitation Center; Formerly, Rehabilitation Counselor, Texas State Commission For The Blind; Rehabilitation Counselor, Texas Rehabilitation Commission; Director, Division of Research and Program Development, Virginia State Department of Vocational Rehabilitation. The following are some of the books which Doctor Cull has co-authored and co-edited: *Drug Dependence and Rehabilitation Approaches, Fundamentals of Criminal Behavior and Correctional Systems, Rehabilitation of the Drug Abuser With Delinquent Behavior,* and *Therapeutic Needs of the Family.* Doctor Cull has contributed more than sixty publications to the professional literature in psychology and rehabilitation.

RICHARD E. HARDY, Ed.D.: Diplomate in Counseling Psychology, Professor and Chairman, Department of Rehabilitation Counseling, Virginia Commonwealth University, Richmond, Virginia; Technical Consultant, United States Department of Health, Education and Welfare, Rehabilitation Services Administration, Washington, D.C.; Editor, American Lecture Series in Social and Rehabilitation Psychology, Charles C Thomas, Publisher; and Associate Editor, *Journal of Voluntary Action Research,* formerly Rehabilitation Counselor in Virginia, Rehabilitation Advisor, Rehabilitation Services Administration, United States Department of Health, Education and Welfare, Washington, D.C., former Chief Psychologist and Supervisor of Professional Training, South Carolina Department of Rehabilitation and member of the South Carolina State Board of Examiners in Psychology. The following are some of the Books which Doctor Hardy has co-authored and co-edited: *Drug Dependence and Rehabilitation Approaches, Fundamentals of Criminal Behavior and Correctional Systems, Rehabilitation of the Drug Abuser with Deliquent Behavior* and *Therapeutic Needs of the Family.* Doctor Hardy has contributed more than sixty publications to the professional literature in psychology and rehabilitation.

GILBERT L. INGRAM, Ph.D.: Associate Director, Federal Youth Center, Englewood, Colorado. Formerly, Coordinator, Mental

Health Programs and Chief Psychologist, Federal Correctional Institution, Tallahassee, Florida; Adjunct Lecturer, Department of Psychology, Florida State University; Consultant, Georgia State Department of Family and Children Services, Waycross Regional Youth Development Center; Book Reviewer, Correctional Psychologist. Formerly, Chief Psychologist, Robert F. Kennedy Youth Center, Adjunct Assistant Professor, West Virginia University, Instructor, Alderson-Broaddus College, Chief Psychologist, National Training School for Boys, and Research Project Director, Federal Bureau of Prisons. Dr. Ingram also has contributed numerous articles to the professional literature in correctional psychology, crime and delinquency.

E. RAY JERKINS, B.A., M.A.: George Peabody College, Nashville, Tennessee; an additional year of Graduate work at Vanderbilt University, Nashville, Tennessee; Clinical Member of the American Association of Marriage and Family Counselors, The National Alliance For Family Life and The American Association of Clinical Counselors; serves on the Board of the National Alliance For Family Life; Past President of the Tennessee Council on Family Relations.

JAY KOONCE: Mr. Koonce attended Centenary College of Louisiana, the University of Texas, Arlington, and Memphis State University where he received his B.A. degree. He has had extensive experience in the psychotherapeutic modalities of Gestalt, Transactional Analysis and Neo-Reichian body work in individual, ongoing group, and weekend marathon settings. After nine years in publishing with major commercial houses, he is returning to school for advanced degrees in clinical psychology.

JOSEPH N. MERTZ, ACSW: Currently Director of Professional Services, The Workshop Inc., Rehabilitation Center, Menands, New York. Mr. Mertz received his B.A. and M.A. in Sociology, Siena College, Loudonville, New York, and his M.S. in Social Work, Columbia University, New York City. Formerly, with the New York State Department of Mental Hygiene in both a State Hospital setting and as Administrator of traveling Child Guidance Clinics; Chief Psychiatric Social Worker and Administrator— Community Mental Health Clinics; Supervisor of Social Services in two local family service agencies. Mr. Mertz is in private practice, part-time in marriage counseling, emotional disturbances in children and adults and is consultant to clinics and social agencies on private level.

ROBERTA E. MALOUF, M.A.: Ms. Malouf is a staff psychologist at the Granite Community Mental Health Center in Salt Lake City and a doctoral candidate in clinical psychology at the University of Utah. In addition to family therapy her research interests include psycholinguistics and child development. She has authored several convention papers and published in *Developmental Psychology* and *Child Development*.

ALBERTO C. SERRANO, M.D.: Director, Community Guidance Center of Bexar County, Texas; Clinical Professor of Psychiatry and Pediatrics and Director, Child and Adolescent Psychiatry, University of Texas Health Science Center at San Antonio.

MARJORIE KAWIN TOOMIM, Ph.D.: Dr. Toomim received her Doctorate from the University of Southern California. She has held several positions of responsibility in the Los Angeles area. Currently Dr. Toomim is in private practice. Her areas of interests are in community, psychology, child development, humanistic psychology and separation counseling.

HELEN C. ZUSNE, Ph.D.: Dr. Zusne received her B.A. degree from Michigan State University and her M.S. and Ph.D. with majors in Clinical Psychology from Purdue University. Her clinical experience includes work at a state neuropsychiatric hospital, a child guidance clinic and a day treatment center. Currently she is in Tulsa, Oklahoma, in private practice which consists of family and marriage counseling, and psychotherapy with children and adults.

This book is dedicated to:

Dr. Roger C. Du Mars
Mobile, Alabama
and Dr. Vernon B. Fox
Tallahassee, Florida

for their many contributions as high level professional practitioners and helping persons.

The following books have appeared thus far in The Social and Rehabilitation Psychology Series:

VOCATIONAL REHABILITATION: PROFESSION AND PROCESS
John G. Cull and Richard E. Hardy

CONTEMPORARY FIELD WORK PRACTICES IN REHABILITATION
John G. Cull and Craig R. Colvin

SOCIAL AND REHABILITATION SERVICES FOR THE BLIND
Richard E. Hardy and John G. Cull

FUNDAMENTALS OF CRIMINAL BEHAVIOR AND
CORRECTIONAL SYSTEMS
John G. Cull and Richard E. Hardy

MEDICAL AND PSYCHOLOGICAL ASPECTS OF DISABILITY
A. Beatrix Cobb

DRUG DEPENDENCE AND REHABILITATION APPROACHES
Richard E. Hardy and John G. Cull

INTRODUCTION TO CORRECTION REHABILITATION
Richard E. Hardy and John G. Cull

VOLUNTEERISM: AN EMERGING PROFESSION
John G. Cull and Richard E. Hardy

APPLIED VOLUNTEERISM IN COMMUNITY DEVELOPMENT
Richard E. Hardy and John G. Cull

VOCATIONAL EVALUATION FOR REHABILITATION SERVICES
Richard E. Hardy and John G. Cull

ADJUSTMENT TO WORK: A GOAL OF REHABILITATION
John G. Cull and Richard E. Hardy

SPECIAL PROBLEMS IN REHABILITATION
A. Beatrix Cobb

DECIDING ON DIVORCE: PERSONAL AND FAMILY
CONSIDERATIONS
John G. Cull and Richard E. Hardy

ACHIEVING CREATIVE DIVORCE: SOCIAL AND PSYCHOLOGICAL
APPROACHES
Richard E. Hardy and John G. Cull

THERAPEUTIC NEEDS OF THE FAMILY: PROBLEMS,
DESCRIPTIONS AND THERAPEUTIC APPROACHES
John G. Cull and Richard E. Hardy

PREFACE

THE QUESTION, "Is the American Family in danger?" is being asked over and over. Many social scientists feel that young people are coming of age at a time when the extended family is already doomed. Changes of a most profound nature are taking place throughout America in family life. Life styles of many young couples are bringing about major changes to what has been called the nuclear family—parents and their children.

Other persons have felt that the family is not dying but is simply adapting to a way of life of the Twentieth Century. The number of weddings has risen from 1,523,000 in 1960 to an estimated 2,160,000 in 1971.

There are many factors which are influencing current day marriages and family life. For example, young wives are working in much higher percentages than their mothers did. Nearly half of all wives in their early 20's are now employed. Young women are often much less satisfied to spend their lives doing housework than they once were. Many feel that being the career housewife is not fully satisfying.

In 1920 the divorce rate was one for every seven marriages. In 1940 it was one for every six marriages; in 1960, according to U.S. Census Bureau, there was one divorce for every five marriages and that figure has now moved to 1 divorce for every three marriages.

Why are so many families disintegrating? It seems that most divorces which occur do so in conflicts over money and sex. Recent studies have shown that seventy to eighty percent of all marriages are plagued by problems relating to sex.

All practitioners know that as the wife begins to work a strain is created in that the family's hierarchy is upset. The wife becomes more independent and her husband is often threatened in terms of his leadership role. In addition, household duties and responsibilities per family member become confused.

Many persons are now overemphasizing the importance of totally satisfactory sexual relationships in deciding whether or not to remain together. It is true that in the past the marriage was viewed primarily as a way of producing and rearing children and sexual enjoyment was not as highly essential as it seems to have become in a society which may be overly sexually oriented. This has been particularly profound in recent years especially as evidenced by the 1971 Gallup poll which showed that nearly two-thirds of all college students had had premarital sex. One partner's shortcomings in performance may cause guilt and feelings of inadequacy for him while great disappointment can begin to develop for the other partner. Some of these factors and others, including the trend of enjoying much coveted freedom in terms of few or no children, the increasing interest in abortion and male sterilization, as well as increased technological advances in contraception, are bringing about marked changes in attitudes and ways of life among people. We may be now seeing the results of the lessened emphasis on family life in many of the juvenile delinquents that we are dealing with in counseling and therapy sessions. Certainly we will see more of this in the future.

RICHARD E. HARDY
JOHN G. CULL

Richmond, Virginia

CONTENTS

MARITAL AND FAMILY COUNSELING

Chapter 1

MARITAL COUNSELING: GOALS AND DIMENSIONS

RICHARD E. HARDY AND JOHN G. CULL

• •

INTRODUCTION

RAPID SOCIAL CHANGE

WHAT IS MARITAL COUNSELING?

INDIVIDUAL ROLE CHANGE

RESPONSIBILITIES OF THE COUNSELOR

REFERENCES

• •

INTRODUCTION

FEW COUNSELORS who are concerned in the broad areas of social services, including psychiatry, rehabilitation, education, the ministry, social work, and/or psychology, can do their work without becoming involved at times with their clients' marital problems. The entire field of marital counseling could be described as a very recent addition to the social service helping field and, for this reason, there is considerable ambiguity concerning its dimensions and who is qualified to practice.

The marital counselor faces many difficult problems with

his clients. He will not give them direct advice concerning what they should do to solve various problems, but he will work with them on a one-to-one basis, in husband-wife sessions and/or in group helping situations in order to explore various approaches to problem solving. The counselor must have considerable information for ready use. This information concerns family stability, feelings, budgets, attitudes, sexual beliefs, marital roles and others.

RAPID SOCIAL CHANGE

Our society is experiencing so much change at such a fast pace that adjustment to change itself is becoming a social problem. This rapid social change, which includes, of course, attitudes of all of us concerning moral values, ethics and family behavior, is changing life in America and throughout much of the world. Institutions, such as the church, the family, governmental structures of service, the university and other educational systems, are changing so rapidly that many persons are losing their anchor points for emotional stability. People look around them and find little or no certainty in their jobs, their family life, or the traditional and religious beliefs formerly held sacrosanct. All of us are deeply influenced by the effects of the mass media such as television. These media depict to us what the outside world seems to be doing. In many cases persons outside of our world seem to be involved in many exciting activities. Many people live vicariously, and some people wish to change their life patterns and family structure in order to relieve boredom and go "where the action is." This immature approach to achieving goals seldom brings happiness.

With an increased amount of leisure time and a de-emphasis on full work days and work weeks, many persons are finding difficulty in managing their personal lives. The changing social environment in which we live has forced the marital counselor into a role of increased importance as a social service professional. His responsibilities affect individuals, their families, their work, leisure and enjoyment, and their hopes for personal stability.

WHAT IS MARITAL COUNSELING?

Counseling has been defined in various terms and by many experts. Gustad (1953) has written that "Counseling is a learning oriented process, carried on in a simple, one-to-one social environment in which a counselor, professionally competent in relative psychological skills and knowledge, seeks to assist the client to learn more about himself, to know how to put understanding into effect in relation to clearly perceived, realistically defined goals to the end that the client may be a happier and more productive member of his society."

While definitions vary according to the orientation of the counselor, certain truisms have resulted from the enormous amount of research concerning the effectiveness of counseling. These will be explained in the following paragraphs.

No matter what particular school or theory of counseling is accepted by the practitioner, the most important factor for determining the outcome of counseling effectiveness is the "personality" of the counselor himself. In other words, whether he counts himself as Rogerian, Ellisonian or eclectic, the personality of the counselor will come through in counseling sessions and affect the outcome to a degree which will determine whether or not the counseling session is effective. Just as teachers can bring about enormous growth and changes in students by modifying their attitudes toward various subject matter, the marital counselor can bring about substantial changes in his clients for better or for worse.

Effective counseling requires certain basic ingredients. As the strength or weakness of these ingredients vary so does the ability of the counselor to be effective with the client. There are three basic prerequisites to effective counseling. First, the counselor must accept the client without imposing conditions for this acceptance. He must be willing to work with the client and become actively involved with him as an individual, no matter what may be the counselee's race, attitudes, or mode of life. This is necessary in order for the counselee to gain the knowledge that the counselor as a person wishes to help him with his problems and is not prejudging.

Secondly, the counselor must be "genuine" in that he must function in a way which indicates to the client that he is being true to his own feelings and to himself. To be otherwise is to present a facade to the client—a false image which will act as a deterrent to a successful relationship. Counselors must avoid artificiality in their relationships. If the counselor hides behind a professional mystique, he may find that the counselee is better at "fooling" him than he is at deceiving the client. The professional worker cannot expect his client to be open, sincere, or genuine if he himself does not represent these characteristics well.

Finally, the counselor must have an empathic understanding and feeling vis-a-vis the client. He must make a sincere effort to see the client's problems through the client's eyes, and he must be able to communicate the depth of his understanding.

Marital counseling can be considered a relationship between two or more persons which is conducive to good mental health. Inherent in an effective counseling relationship is the absence of threat. The counselor must remove threat if the client is to grow and be able to solve his problems in an uninhibited manner. Counseling as a relationship is also typified by the feelings many of us have for our closest friends. True close friendships are characterized by honest caring, genuine interest and a high level of concern about helping in a time of need. Real friendships often require one person to put aside his own selfish needs in order to listen long enough with enough empathy that a friend's problem may begin to work itself out in a natural and constructive manner.

Marital counseling services vary according to the needs of the client—not the counselor. Often, when a counselee comes to the counselor for help, he at first will outline a concern which is not the real problem. The counselor must have considerable flexibility and insight in order to know what is required in each individual situation and the appropriate responses for given situations.

The counselor in a marital session always has the goal of bringing about change in the marital relationship. Marital counseling may be effective in helping clients to decide whether

or not they can "live" with their situation as it is, to change
that situation without separation, to separate for a period of
time, to divorce. All these alternatives are realistic possibilities
for end results in successful marital counseling.

Any solution short of total reconciliation is generally considered by our society as indicative of personal failure. This
very fact inhibits many people in their exploration of possibilities other than total reconciliation. Many persons fall in line
with society's enforced rules and regulations in the past virtually forcing many persons to remain in unhappy and malad-
justed marital situations. That going for help, to a marital
counselor for personal adjustment or to a lawyer in order to
discuss legal aspects of separation and divorce, is also indicative of personal shortcomings is the attitude of many persons in society in general. Relatives, peer persons and groups
put enormous pressure on the individuals concerned to go
back together at all "costs." This "getting back together,"
in effect, saves the family from what some people think of as
"disgrace" and makes both family and friends feel more comfortable. Every counselor must take into consideration and
impart to his clients the knowledge that, while many friends
and relatives wish to help, their first thoughts concern what
they would like to see as an end result of the consideration
rather than what is necessarily best for the partners in difficulty.

Due to strong societal conformity pressure and the problems
which individuals have after threatened or actual separation
or divorce, they particularly need counseling. Counseling may
be concerned with actual problems or anticipated problems
of the separation or divorce and the reaction of the individual
to the threatened or terminated marriage; or there may be
a combination of both of these problem areas.

INDIVIDUAL ROLE CHANGE

Societal change is now fast paced and affects roles which
individuals have in marital situations as they experience various
aspects of their lives and develop new interests and maturity.
A common myth holds that the well adjusted person in our

society is one who experiences many worldly things but does not change. All people change, and generally change is for the best in terms of an individual's increased maturity. It is important for husband and wife to discuss the redefining of roles which often comes about as each grows, matures, and changes in interests. If such discussions are held on a frank basis, many questions concerning changes in sexual behavior, business activities, attitudes concerning the importance of work, family entertaining, housekeeping, etc., can be understood more fully.

Role confusion concerning the wife and mother is now profound. Many women no longer are satisfied to devote their entire lives to family life. Many feel insecure as they see the marriages of their peers "breaking up" with increased regularity. More and more women wish to be self-supporting and self-sufficient and do not wish to relegate themselves to what has been called "housewifery." This fact also can readily threaten the male who has carried the image of himself as the total bread earner and, in many cases, the master of his domain. The husband often can misconceive the working role of the wife as one of competition and one which can be a threat to his marriage due to the many new contacts his wife will experience in work. Her work and his reaction to it can affect greatly whether or not additional children are added to the family unit.

We cannot overstress the importance of periodically discussing and defining roles during the years of marriage. People are now living longer. At one time when the last child left home it was near to the time for both husband and wife to die. Today parents experience a new adjustment period, in that life continues for many more years after the children have left home. There has been no societal definition of roles for middle-aged and older couples. We are seeing now an increase in the number of persons being divorced once the "nest is empty."

RESPONSIBILITIES OF THE COUNSELOR

The counselor must be certain that confidentiality of the marital counseling relationship is maintained and the client must understand this feeling. This includes the counselor's being involved in possible court testimony at a later date. The counselor must let it be known to his clients and others that he cannot have an effective counseling relationship if either client feels that he is not completely free to discuss various feelings and experiences. Clients must have a clear sense of security.

Counselors come from all segments of society and represent various ages, races, sexes, and religions. Each of them has experienced a variety of conflicts and problems of the same types which trouble their clients. The difference between the client and the counselor (helpee and helper) is that the client is experiencing difficulty and, for the most part, counselors feel that their own handicaps and problems are under control. The counselor must guard against automatic feelings of superiority and should see himself as an individual who also has difficulties and who simply wishes to help another individual work his way through problems.

The counselor must be able to recognize when he should refer clients to other counselors or sources of help. There may be problems of countertransference which interfere with the counseling relationship. Race, age, sex, and religion almost invariably affect the counseling outcomes. For instance, counselors who are older may be out of touch with some of the problems of the younger generation, or male counselors may not fully understand the emerging role of the female in today's society. Counselors who have strong religious beliefs may be unable to offer unbiased information, and those with racial biases and prejudices may experience difficulties of an obvious nature.

Counselors must be certain that they have received adequate training and supervision. Academic requirements in terms of five or six years of college and at least two degrees should have been completed. Supervision in counseling practice, as a part of academic and later training, is also most important. Each counselor should continue professional growth by active involvement in appropriate professional organizations (according to his interests and trainings). Examples are the American Psychological Association and the American Association of Marriage and Family Counselors. Ethical codes of conduct of these organizations should be strictly followed.

Again, the counselor must guard against the temptation to play "God." Generally, counselors who use directive and authoritarian approaches are exposed over and over to rationalizations of their own dictatorial motives.

As indicated earlier the personality of the counselor is the decisive factor in the success or failure of therapeutic activities. Counselors constantly must evaluate their own behavior and attitudes toward their work in general and their clients in particular. The counselor must remember that he is working toward the development of the client's ability to make future satisfactory decisions and to achieve a mature dependability.

REFERENCES

Gustad, J. W.: The definition of counseling. In Berdie, R. F.: *Roles and Relationships in Counseling.* Minneapolis, U of Minn Pr, 1953.

CHAPTER 2

DIVORCE AS A FINAL OPTION IN FAMILY PSYCHOTHERAPY

JOSEPH CASSIUS AND JAY KOONCE

●●●

●●●

INTRODUCTION

ANALYSIS OF NATIONWIDE statistics shows that our divorce rate has been rising from the end of the Civil War to the present. In 1867 it stood at one divorce for every thirty-six marriages, in 1900 at one for twelve marriages, in 1945 at one for three. Current estimates suggest a divorce rate of one divorce for four marriages. In the 1970's in California, usually a harbinger of national trends, the rate is about one divorce for every two marriages among the general population and in urban centers as high as four for five. Similar, and sometimes higher, divorce rates are found in other countries experiencing a rapid or high degree of industrialization.

It is important to state that the frequency of a condition does not make it healthy. The truth of this assertion is obvious when one considers how many times parties, who turn to divorce as a solution to unhappiness, fail to experience an increment in happiness and often become more confused, depressed and dissatisfied with life than before. Seemingly for these, divorce was an incomplete, if not an inappropriate solution. Alternatives to divorce, however, are not within the scope of this chapter. We are concerned here with determining when the most appropriate relief from a destructive relationship is a divorce. We would add that there is probably no acceptable way of defining either a "healthy" marriage or a "healthy" divorce anymore than there is of defining "mental health."

LANGUAGE AND FUNCTION OF TRANSACTIONAL ANALYSIS

In our experience with psychotherapy we have found that the language and principles of Transactional Analysis (TA), developed by Dr. Eric Berne, greatly facilitate communication and understanding among all the members, children as well as adults, of a family in the process of a separation or divorce. Dr. Franklin Ernst, a prominent psychiatrist and leading proponent of TA, reports that children as young as three years old have learned the language of TA. Due to the high popularity of *Games People Play* by Dr. Berne and *I'm OK, You're OK* by Dr. Thomas Harris, many people are familiar with TA terminology; but for those who are not, we will include a brief discussion of terms and principles which may appear throughout this chapter:

> *Structural Analysis:* the interrelationship of the three discrete parts, Parent (*P*), Adult (*A*) and Child (*C*), of the individual personality.
>
> *Transactional Analysis:* the interrelationship of the *PAC* of one person with that of another.

Parent: the ego state that is an incorporation of the feelings, behavior and attitudes of one's real parents. Behavior that is either prejudicial (demanding, critical) or nurturing is displayed by the individual from this state.

Adult: the ego state that gathers data from the other internal ego states and the external world, subjects it to reality testing, probability estimation, and logical computation and chooses the most appropriate course of behavior. An internal computer.

Child: the ego state that is intuitive, creative, feeling, sensuous, fun-loving. It can be "natural," free from the influence of the internal parent ("I want what I want when I want it"), or "adapted," either acceding to or defying the demands of the internal Parent but, either way, subject to its influence.

Paul McCormick effectively and simply describes how these ego states relate to each other and the environment to make a most important decision:

> As an infant develops into childhood he uses his computer to gather data about where he fits in his world, and by age five or six he has probably arrived at an enduring decision. Perhaps even earlier than that he has concluded, both cognitively and by way of feelings, that he is either essentially lovable or unlovable (depending on whether his parents love him), and that other people are, by and large, either lovable or unlovable (depending again on his nurturers' example setting). Although there are an infinite number of degrees between lovability and unlovability, people seem to have adopted a life stance that is more toward one end of the continuum than the other.[1]

As a result of where he positions himself on this continuum, he formulates, with varying degrees of detail, a basic position from which he will live his life and a plan for living that is congruent with this position. This is called a *script.*

---

[1] Paul McCormick, "Guide For Use with a Life Script," Questionnaire in *Transactional Analysis,* (Berkeley, Transactional Publications, 1971) p. 2.

Since the script is based upon early relationships of the individual, there is a good possibility that it may impose unnecessary restrictions upon the range and quality of later relationships and become the source of frustration and anxiety. A person adopts and maintains his script in order to insure that he will receive at least the minimum *stroking* necessary to sustain life. *Strokes* may be physical or symbolic (a look, a smile, a word) and fulfill the nurturing function of affirming the fact of one's existence. One's script may be directed toward positive strokes (reinforcement of a position of OK'ness) or negative strokes (reinforcement of a position of not OK'ness), but, in either case, the important point is that stroking affirms that one simply is. While one plays out his script he is assured of this affirmation, this recognition. This is why it is so difficult to remove the negative aspects of a person's script, to alter his script in any way, because doing so means taking a risk that the new script will not afford sufficient stroking to sustain life. Scripts can be changed, however, since they were the result of a decision on the part of the individual, early in life, that this would be the best way for him to encounter the world.

Leonard Campos explains the function of scripts in marriage as follows:

> Your marriage is based on an ulterior Child-to-Child contract, required by each of your scripts. This agreement, perhaps outside of your Adult awareness, determined your choice of marital partner. Your two scripts are probably *complementary*. Both of you had different sets of parents, so necessarily you have two different scripts. But you have fit the two together for more than Adult reasons. Life scripts are complementary when the injunctions of two persons match. For example, a man whose script calls for a dominant-male role will be attracted to a woman whose script calls for a submissive-female role. In structuring time for strokes with others, you will be attracted to persons who play complementary game roles required by your script (and vice versa). Most married couples have complementary scripts.[2]

---

[2] Leonard Campos and Paul McCormick, *Introduce Your Marriage to TA: A Primer* (Stockton, San Joaquin TA Institute, 1972), p. 27.

By using TA you can disentangle from your relationship those parental script instructions on marriage that you have been following without Adult awareness. You can change what your script calls for, or *rescript* your marriage in your own way. If you do, you will feel a pull toward behavior and feelings required by your old script. And you may have a struggle in freeing yourself from the old ways of early family dramas. In your Child you may be reluctant to give up your customary ways of getting stroked, not being sure that a new way will work.[3]

TA IN COUNSELING BEFORE DIVORCE

When one, or both, of the partners in a marriage is unwilling or "unable" to make the adjustments necessary to have complementary scripts, is unwilling to give up the games that produce mutually destructive negative strokes, then divorce can be examined as a means of finding the freedom needed to get on with a productive life. The script of each party may be individually constructive and yet the combination may be noncomplementary, thus requiring an alteration of the script of at least one to achieve a complementary script relationship and, hopefully, a harmonious marriage, separation, or divorce.

We will propose that the healthy divorce would be a separation between two adults whose scripts could not be made to fit without serious damage to one or the other participant. It is not an uncommon observation that many marriages in which tremendous self-destruction occurs may remain relatively stable. This is due to a resistance to an alteration of their basic life attitudes, their scripts, necessary for a healthy relationship. Obviously our definition of healthy is already prejudiced. We believe there are certain combinations of personalities which inevitably produce tragic results. Yet there is no denying that for many of us tragedy is one of the important accomplishments in life. Destroying or being destroyed may be the only meaningful experience in an otherwise meaningless life.

Where children are involved, our society designates families from which one parent is missing, because of divorce, as broken. The concept of breakage suggests a loss of cohesion, of order

---

[3] Ibid., p. 29.

and, where an organism is involved, a loss of function. The concept of "broken family" implies that a member of a family system is missing and that a separation has come about through an act of destructiveness.

An important part of mate selection is choosing a partner who will "fit in" with one's script, and as children are born they quickly take supporting roles congruent with the couple's ongoing life drama. Each member of the family is an integral part of the family system, and the loss of one member, for whatever reason, can be extremely disruptive and confusing to the remaining members of the family system.

In order to minimize insecurity and maximize freedom for all concerned, Marjorie Kawin Toomin (1972) recommends a structured separation, a voluntary separation prior to a "have to" separation, to help avoid manipulation and mistrust. Her work involved a three-month trial separation period during which the whole family was involved in counseling. The couple agreed to live apart with no binding financial, legal, or custody arrangements. Each party was to have the freedom to explore relationships with other people so that, if their decision was for reconciliation, the implication of a voluntary preference of each for the other over other potential choices provides positive strokes and enhances their self-concept.

An emphasis is placed upon change and risk and loss: how one feels about loss; how one replaces the loss; an awareness of the need to mourn the loss; realization that the loss must become finished business. How to make the change is as important as the change itself. There is an emphasis upon developing a choice between positives instead of between a negative and the unkown. The family members become aware that they had dependency needs and control needs that were met by the missing member, and this period of separation gives them an opportunity to explore other ways to meet these needs or to decide that they are willing, if these needs are important enough, to overlook some liabilities of the departed member so that he can stay within the family and maintain his role. The continuance of the family's script can be maintained only if all the cast members are present, if someone else can assume the missing role, or if the drama is changed. If such an alternative effort still fails to produce the necessary adjustments required to establish complementary scripts then divorce becomes a viable option.

Divorce can be a positive act of creation, marking the end of a period of impasse in which realization of potential has been static, due to maintenance of patterns of existence perpetuated by familiar games, past-times, and rituals which do not allow one to achieve the risky position that can launch them into growth. Mutually reinforcing inertia and ennui drain one of the energy needed for living a vital life, for actualizing potentials. The effort required to maintain an attitude of constant vigilance, lest one should have to confront the reality that the marriage has become an endless exercise in the avoidance of intimacy, is draining physically as well as emotionally.

The couple has gone from avoidance of intimacy to the further remove of avoidance of the admission of the avoidance of intimacy, for this admission would only exacerbate the guilt inherent therein. This guilt is a product of having to admit to failure, to having made a mistake, and, since reward (acceptance) increases in direct proportion to degree of perfection, and, since failure is met not only with decreased reward or non-reward, but often with anti-reward (punishment or rejection), and, as long as the parties involved can use devices which allow them to ignore their failure, trying to escape the confrontation of rejection.

In reality, however, this process of complex Byzantine machinations leads to rejection of self, which is inescapable except through such extreme measures as suicide or psychosis. For the failure is a part of one's total real essence, and to suppress any part of one's reality is to distort it all. In order to grow, and to cease growing is to cease living, one must build on the foundation of his own reality, and, if a marriage requires the suppression of this reality, then both partners are stifled and so is the marriage.

One must first know himself, get in touch and maintain contact with his own reality and accept this real self,—both assets and liabilities—if he is to achieve any degree of emotional fulfillment. He then needs to be willing to disclose this self to his partner. There should be mutual disclosures or they will be living with strangers, only shadows of reality with little substance. And a marriage based on such ephemera must unavoidably be dubious, vague, and unreal. Awareness and acceptance of self and disclosure of that self are necessary to any true, vital relationship. Energy formerly used to maintain "protective" subterfuge can then be released for self-actualization.

When serious attempts to revitalize a stagnant, destructive relationship have proved unsatisfactory, when all other feasible options are exhausted, it is time to consider divorce as the final option. Partners should first try to save themselves, and, if in the process, the marriage is saved, well and good. When partners in a marriage (either one or both) realize that to pursue a life-goal, based on their awareness of their real selves (a goal which is emotionally and physically healthy), will require life styles that are incompatible, then divorce can be a creative, productive release.

Often people, when told of the decision to divorce on the part of friends, respond by saying that they only want the best for both parties. If what one party thinks is best for him limits or restricts his partner's potential for personal fulfillment, then to maintain the marriage is not the best for both; in fact, it cannot even be the best for the one who thinks it is, for, if his stifled partner could be released, he would have the opportunity to find a new partner who might be even more gratifying. Insistence on living with a person whose fulfillment is inhibited by the bonds of matrimony means sharing life with a dissatisfied, unhappy mate, and the sum of this union cannot entail moments of optimal happiness. One plus less-than-one cannot sum to two.

When a marriage, then, has reached an unresolvable impasse in terms of freedom for individual growth and thus mutual growth, divorce becomes the final option, the only really healthy, acceptable option. If fear of giving up the familiar misery incumbent in the marriage (a paradox of comfort-discomfort) and the tenuous ease of preferring known failures over risking being unable to cope with possible new ones, can be overcome, the marriage can be dissolved, and debilitating, inhibiting components of the old life style can be excised, and liberating, facilitating new ones can be added.

FAMILY COUNSELING DURING AND AFTER DIVORCE

It is the function of the professional therapist to help in discovering these new directions and illuminating the appropriate means for achieving them. He can help the ex-partners and other family members get in touch with themselves on multiple levels: awareness of one's body, kinship to nature and mankind, richness of emotions, marvels of mental processes. An awareness of the points of commonality with other beings can serve as a foundation for appreciation and celebration of those traits which delineate his uniqueness, for a sense of self-worth is enhanced by both commonality and individuality. The psychotherapist must guide the person foundering in the throes of divorce, separation, rejection, and guilt through the steps to self-acceptance, self-protection, and self-worth.

The first phenomenon which occurs following separation is one of shock. This is ordinarily more profound and longer lasting in the woman than in the man; in fact, for some men this initial stage may be so brief as to be completely missed by an outside observer. Following shock, which is usually manifested by immobility of affect and activity, there occurs some manifestation of anger. This may be suicidal behavior, rampant acting-out of destructive impulses toward the self or the other, or, under the best circumstances, it is channeled into rejection of the other person. During this stage, the task is to bring into awareness all of the elements in the other person which are hated and which are unacceptable to the individual. This has the concomitant effect of reestablishing and reclarifying the identity of the individual in therapy. The mutual expression of hatred helps to redefine the personalities and reestablish the life scripts. It is during this stage of mutual rejection and hatred that legal action is most appropriate. The law is a creation of mankind which has been evolved to provide some rational basis for dealing with the most irrational experiences in life.

During this stage of structural realignment, it is important for each of the individuals to obtain a fair assessment of each one's desires in the course of the separation. When a professional helper is involved, very often his task is to support in the struggle for equitable treatment. At times transactions of a helping nature are rejected because they seem inappropriate in terms of a disrupted self-concept. At other times these transactions are accepted because they correspond to parts of the self-concept which we might label as distorted or neurotic.

The family itself is a complex system of transactional relationships. Therefore a broken family is really a closed system of mutually acceptable transactions which has been broken open by the departure of one member of that system. When this departure is occasioned by divorce, a sequence of rearrangements of the system is inevitable. The remaining members of a broken family have, therefore, in addition to their traditional functions (or roles in the family script), a repair function to perform and have to do this after the experience of weakening which always follows destruction.

The feelings of overwhelming defeat and failure involved in divorce can lead the individuals to fail to adequately recognize their own value. The law reflects this universal problem of self-devaluation and recognizes that it is the woman who is most likely to suffer these consequences. Therefore, the law generally provides for full and complete protection of the basic rights of the woman to equitable treatment. The value she has under the law should lend positive support to her own self-concept.

During this stage of the separation process, whether it be divorce, death, or any other type of separation, the parties may experience inner signals which can lead toward appropriate and meaningful future development. This has been clearly observed by us while sharing clients' separation experiences in psychotherapy. When the individual is involved in a therapeutic relationship, the use of Gestalt dream psychotherapy during the year following separation can be tremendously helpful in discovering the appropriate pathways for the individual to pursue, to activate his Adult. All of the well-known games, such as "Look how bad I've got it," "If it weren't for you," "Stupid," "Kick me," etc., as well as the compulsion to repeat the same destructive life script that led him here can be seen operating during this period. If the person can marshal sufficiently strong positive sources of energy to reintegrate his personality (his Adult, particularly) at a high level of self-awareness and consciousness, then he or she is able to advance to a new stage in life and modify the basic script. Some persons have a particularly difficult time establishing anything other than a dependency relationship (seeing their opposites as Prejudiced Parent or Nurturing Parent) and have trouble reestablishing Adult to Adult or Child to Child transactions.

The likelihood of the need for strengthening intervention by a therapist is inherent in divorce. This need may exist independent of the character of the divorce, either as a life-failure or as a constructive experience. Whether the divorce is creative or destructive, it must be examined from the point of view of whether it creates the opportunity for growth for the partners and their dependents or whether it is undertaken to fulfill a tragic script. When partners discover their transferences (oedipal or pre-oedipal fantasies) from parent to spouse, they may precipitate unmet expectations and lead to a decision to divorce. The pursuit of these fantasies is obvious evidence of unresolved destructive marital disturbances. Unhealthy divorces can also be based on destructiveness and the wish to hurt and be hurt. One of the most basic fears of many is their Child's fear of being abandoned. If a man insists on a divorce in order to confirm this fear in his wife's Child, his motivation in divorce is destructive. But if this fear exists in her and his motivation in divorce is other than to confirm it, his behavior is still destructive. Behavior can be more relevant here than motivation.

Divorce need not be destructive. When two people discover that their games or defenses are incompatible and interfere with their maintenance of identity and emotional well-being, a divorce can be productive. Life energy requires sustenance, and intimacy must be nurtured, or life-supportive, if a relationship is to be classified as positive. We no longer view our current lives in terms of rewards in life after death regardless of present discomforts. Therefore, paradise becomes within one's reach in the here and now, and, where reality does not sustain here and now pleasure in marriage, the pain of divorce becomes an acceptable choice. Divorce must be more than a "Get Rid Of . . ." solution; It must append "And Get On With. . . ." It should be more than an escape from . . . ; it should be an escape to . . . ; a positive decision.

On a dynamic level, many of us marry to perpetuate the cultural ideal of continued improvement and the conscious or unconscious wish to have a better marriage than our parents. When a marriage does not live up to these expectations of improvement over what Mom and Dad had, termination may occur. On the other hand, people whose parents were divorced sometimes stick to unsatisfactory marriages to establish a variation in identity from their parents. If a marriage is seen as an opportunity for happiness that was not available in one's family, an unsatisfactory marriage may threaten one's self-esteem or image, and one may have to prove that he can have a better marriage than his parents; therefore dissolving the relationship permits a new quest for self-esteem and identity.

Some people seek gratification in another "start," that is, in a second marriage, by surrendering to cultural pressure for remarriage. There is no social solution for the problem of the one unit family, since pressure is put on people to maintain two person units. Homes can function without a father, although child rearing by a single parent is socially awkward. For many, divorce is a regressive experience with the temptation to return home to parents and to engage in dating again. Also, unrealistic fantasies of being able to start again and win back the former spouse will interfere with appropriate adjustment and development.

Clear cut contracts (therapeutic goals) need to be established. Therapy has to resolve the ambivalence regarding the former partner, affect the acceptance of sexual needs and the attainment of adequacy in meeting them, and help the children find substitute models for "reparenting." The parent with whom the children remain has to be liberated from the belief that he must play the role of *two parents* to the children. Since children are demanding, the single parent faces extra burdens. It is impossible for a parent to be a role and identity model for both sexes.

Many get a divorce in order to find a new marriage, yet the fact of divorce signifies a failure in mate selection and a failure in personal communication which the partners could not remedy. This failure exaggerates the non-OK Child position. One has made a mistake and one has been unable to correct it by making the marriage work. Whether one is forced to seek a divorce or has been forced to accept it as the choice of one's partner, the sense of inadequacy in failing will leave one or both partners with feelings of rage against the self or the other. A second chance may be impaired by the devastating impact of the divorce on the partner's self-image. This is true for the second-rounders as well as the person who decides to live without another marriage. Guilt over denying one's presence to the children may be felt and may be increased by the temptation to use the children as pawns in the continued uproar between both parents. Exploitation of the children leads to further buildup of guilt; the victim feels and resents the exploitation (persecution) and, in turn, becomes hostile to the persecutor.

In divorce problems the mother who uses the child to express aggression against her husband (whom she wrongly chose or failed to keep) will ultimately earn the anger of her children and may thus feel doubly deprived or hurt. One parent may try to present himself as being better than the parent with whom the children must live. Children from broken families may be scripted for broken families themselves, thus remaining poor prospects for two person units, just as their parents were, unless remedial intervention is sought. Perpetuation of personality patterns (scripting) from parent to child may extend for several generations, as can be observed by family therapists. Stimulation of destructive urges, which unhappy marriages may produce in children, seems to make the children seek similar relationships (to maintain negative strokes) later in life rather than seek positive strokes through real intimacy.

Therapists can play a vital role in helping divorced parties to make the consequences of their divorce as undamaging as possible for themselves and for their children. First, the therapist can provide the broken family with an opportunity to vent feelings and to understand what has happened to them. An explanation of Structural Analysis and Transactional Diagrams can be especially useful here in helping children to understand what has happened. If children are involved, both spouses may be included in sessions. Family treatment may require the inclusion of the spouse who has left home. One of the areas touched upon may be abuse of visiting rights for the purpose of maintaining games between both ex-marrieds. Family therapy sessions can teach each parent to interact nondestructively, for his own sake as well as that of the children and potential grandchildren. Another thing the helper can do is to help the divorced person repair his self-concept. People with similar problems attract each other but can't cure each other. The seductiveness of someone else with similar misery, anxiety, suffering and hostility may bring relief, but not cure, and may present the possibility of failure in a second marriage. Seeking one with the same personality problems may lead to shattering games, since marriage, like all other human relationships, requires exchange of need satisfaction.

The problem of psychological self-repair and personality growth in response to defeat is demanding. Where a parent is missing, many times the presence of a sibling can be a focal point for family cohesion. The brother's and sister's bonds increase with the additional responsibility added by loss of a parent. The attainment of skills and personality development can be promoted through identification with an older brother or sister. Often a brother or sister, a teacher or a therapist may be successfully used as a role model substitute for a missing parent. The children are taught thru Structural Analysis not to blame themselves for the breakup of a marriage or for not having done more to keep their parents' marriage together. Children can use TA to understand (recognize) what games their parents played and that their parents' personalities were formed and script decisions made before they were born. The parents must help the children to understand and to avoid the same suffering and personality strife which involved their parents.

Once partners understand that divorce can be a beneficial action they need some guidelines for working through the divorce process and beginning their new lives. Some of the ways that this can be done are outlined in the following prescription for a healthy divorce. The list is not exhaustive; the reader can probably make appropriate deletions and additions to fit the circumstances of the moment.

A PRESCRIPTION FOR A HEALTHY DIVORCE

1. Avoid destructive outlets for unavoidable anger by channeling it into rejection of the ex-mate through delineation and excision (in self) of his most unacceptable traits. When you know what you don't want, it helps you find what you do want by narrowing your options.
2. Take necessary legal steps. Accept the protection afforded by the law and gain reaffirmation of personal worth as legal processes reinforce the need for "belongingness." You do belong to society because the law provides for you.
3. Realign your "functional" (where there are children). Accommodation must be made to assume the functions formerly performed by the departing partner. A revised family drama with a revised script must be enacted.
4. Consult a professional helper. Analysis of dreams during the period following separation (in the Perls-Gestalt model) can be helpful in pointing toward new directions in living.
5. Establish new goals. Attain a high level of self-awareness. (Both should be based on real possibilities and limitations.)
6. Develop a "good" self-concept. Improvement of physical image can nurture psychological image.
7. Eliminate unnecessary fears, e.g., a woman can make it in the world and appropriate, opposite-sex models can be found for children.
8. "Own" the failure of divorce and still be OK. "Own" social opprobrium and still be OK.
9. Be concerned with what is good for the children, not what comforts you.
10. Participate in family psychotherapy if appropriate. Help children avoid repeating "scripts" of their parents, and absolve them of whatever guilt they might feel due to the separation.

11. Avoid reentry into marital state with a carbon of your previous partner or with one who mirrors your own problems.

ACKNOWLEDGMENTS

Much of the refinement of TA, both as an effective therapeutic mode and as a theory of personality, is a result of the freedom and openness with which members of the TA community have shared their ideas and practical experiences. We are indebted to and appreciative of the following whom we have known in the various roles of therapist, mentor, author, colleague and friend: Eric Berne, Leonard Campos, Franklin Ernst, Thomas Harris, Muriel James, Dorothy Jongeward, Dave Kupfer, Paul McCormick and Jacqui Lee Schiff. We would also like to acknowledge the contributions to our knowledge and understanding made by clients with whom we have been associated in a psychotherapeutic setting.

REFERENCES

Berne, E.: *What Do You Say After You Say Hello?* New York, Grove, 1972.
Campos, L. and McCormick, P.: *Introduce Your Marriage to TA: A TA Primer*, Stockton, San Joaquin TA Institute, 1972.
Harris, T. A.: *I'M OK—YOU'RE OK*. New York, Har-Row, 1969.
James, M., and Jongeward, D.: *Born to Win: Transactional Analysis with Gestalt Experiments*, Reading, 1971.
McCormick, P.: *Guide For Use with a Life Script Questionnaire in Transactional Analysis*, Berkeley, Transactional Pubs, 1971.
Schiff, J. L. with Day, B.: *All My Children*, New York, Evans, 1971.
Toomin, M. K.: Structured separation with counselling: a therapeutic approach for couples in conflict. *Family Process*, September, 1972, Vol. 2, No. 3.

Chapter 3

SPECIAL COUNSELING PROBLEMS OF MEN

Charles Ansell

•••

INTRODUCTION

LIONEL

DONALD

SPECIAL PROBLEMS OF MEN AFTER DIVORCE

TRAGEDY OF MEN'S DUAL ROLES IN OUR
SOCIETY

•••

INTRODUCTION

I HAD BEEN TALKING with Fred, a lawyer in his mid-forties. He frequently represented clients in divorce proceedings. Our discussion that day turned to the always delicate question of how we, as professional men, understand our own experiences as husbands, as fathers and, sometimes, as divorced men. Fred was divorced over two years ago, but he was currently involved with a woman whom he regarded more seriously than most.

"When I at last realized that Nancy and I were divorcing after fifteen years as man and wife, I knew I had reached a crisis in my life." He turned his head away for an instant, reflecting on some silent thought. "You know," he began, "the Chinese symbol for Crisis is represented by two signs. One reads danger, the other reads opportunity. I had a choice. I took opportunity to resolve my crisis." He smiled widely at his observation. Clearly, Fred had grown since his divorce.

This chapter may well have been titled, not The Special Counseling Problems of Men, but The Special Problems of Fred, Alan, Lionel and Donald. Divorced men may encounter similar experiences, but the differences in their views of these experiences would be too wide to reduce to a set of generalizations. The probability is that Fred, Alan, Lionel, and Don will encounter a sudden loneliness in the first days after the separation, but what each of these men will do to ease the loneliness will vary as widely as their basic personalities. Fred may feel such relief at being free of the oppressive climate of his marriage that his aloneness may never turn to loneliness. Lionel, on the other hand, chronically unsure of himself, uncertain of his decisions, fearful that, in losing Ellen, he had lost all of his potential as a man among women, will proceed to spend his evenings at the telephone calling his old friends to complain tearfully, to strip himself bare emotionally until he reduces his friends to uttering empty banalities. "Pull yourself together Lionel. Lionel it's only temporary. You'll meet other women soon. . . ." "But," (Lionel is prepared for all that.) "How did I fail Ellen? How?"

Despite the wide differences in personality between Fred and Lionel and their characteristic ways of living in a crisis, there remain certain observations that, statistically at least, point to several generalizations about men after divorce. Young men under 25 years of age, who marry early and divorce soon after, encounter a widely different post-divorce life than men over 34. Younger men, for reasons not relevant here, may unconsciously view their erstwhile marriage as a date stretched out too long. Divorce comes easy. A quick return to dating nurtures the illusion that little of serious consequence has occurred. Divorce to the young does not come often with the ominous feeling of crisis. Perhaps divorce for the young lacks the content of crisis-anxiety which older men find in divorce.

This is not to deny that the young can not know crisis; this is only to aver that the nature of crisis is perceived differently between the under 25 and over 34. It would be tempting to turn aside for the moment to ponder the question of which of the two reactions to divorce is, or should be, the "norm." Should it be the seeming casualness of men under 25 or the often crisis-shaken reaction of men over 34? In either case, the reaction to divorce does not descend as a moral problem with its attendant preoccupation with remorse and guilt. Nor would the crisis, which divorce often poses, be resolved by a reordering of moral perspectives. Most often, the crisis reaction to divorce carries the special sting of personal failure. For many men, failure at a task in which they meant to succeed, indeed in which they felt they were expected to succeed, can drop them to despair. The young man, on the other hand, may not suffer his divorce in such stark failure terms as he might if he were suddenly terminated midway in some special studies leading to a career. The nature of distress, felt most acutely by the younger man, rises from an abrupt frustration of private fantasies, fantasies more related to his personal conquest of his world than to the fantasies related to self-enrichment through marriage and family.

Again, the crisis of divorce felt by the older man follows upon a marriage that lasted not one or two years but, most often, ten and fifteen years and more. His marriage produced children whom he fathered from infancy into active young people. He was witness to their problems and their experiences from infancy to adolescence and older. His children entered his life and held a central position in his own life's outlook. Clearly the casualties of failure felt in divorce for the older man are in reality the products of having lived intensely with a woman and having lived as father with children whose very lives were shaped by his presence among them. The young man's view of himself and his world is, to borrow from the philosophers, solipsistic. He is self-centered without being selfish. His self-centeredness is not the result of faulty training in character building but rather the function of a society that spares its young from a too early exposure to the tasks of marriage and family building.

Thus when we speak of the Special Problems of Man after divorce we shall speak of failure not only as each man experiences it, but as our industrialized society unwittingly contributes to it. It is important to note here that divorce, *felt* as failure, is *not* failure in fact. Despairing Lionel turned his feeling of failure into a fact of his personal life, while Fred viewed his failure as a caution, as an opportunity, to correct some hidden problem in his character. One man's failure is another man's opportunity. From a clinical viewpoint Lionel's marrying again without first troubling to correct his special problem, marriage counselors would likely agree, would lead him to repeat his first marriage or his second marriage, neither one of which, as we shall note later, corrected his special problem as a man. "He who does not learn from experience is bound to repeat it."

The discussion in this chapter largely views the special problem of divorce among men from the broad perspective of how men are socialized in our culture. Man in his family and man at his work must be profoundly understood if we are to illuminate the special problem of men after divorce. Too often the special problem of men after divorce is simplistically and mistakenly met by urging the recently divorced man to virtually lose himself in a round of activity. This view overlooks, and dangerously so, the inner mood of uncertainty and despair which the divorced man may feel, a despair made the deeper because he is everywhere surrounded by optimistic and enthusiastic reports which he knows are false and, indeed, which his well-wishers only wish were true.

As we shall suggest later in this chapter, men in our culture are poorly prepared for the loving intimacy of marriage and family and this neglect often looms formidably above them after they find themselves divorced. This failure at emotional preparation is, as we shall note, more specially the problem of men than of women, and, because they fail to grasp this insight even after divorce, their problem is great and their pain difficult to explain.

What follows are clinical portraits of two men, Lionel and Donald. Our two studies are of widely different characters, and indeed they may be regarded as exceptional, if not atypical, studies from which to draw generalizations about the special problems of men. Yet within the two studies that follow may be found reliable indications of the special problems of all men. For in the lives of Lionel and Donald there has always been a central plaguing doubt about that which, for want of a precise term, may call Commitment, the freedom to make choices. A divorce of a marriage which is not remembered as having been freely chosen is not, as one would think, release from a yoke of bondage. Men are more often distressed over their failure at matters they did not initiate than over failures in matters they once chose. The Zorba of fiction who looked out at disaster after months of preparation, who saw his efforts crumble at his feet, who laughed at the absurdity of life and proceeded to dance madly amid the rubble, as if by this mad indifference he could defy disaster to possess him completely, is the Zorba of illusion and fiction. There are few Zorbas among divorced men. Even Fred, who appeared stoical after his divorce, found in his divorce the occasion for introspection. The Lionels of this world look out upon their lives as a continuing disaster. Now let us turn to our studies of Lionel and Donald.

LIONEL

Lionel was the only child of immigrant parents. "Ethnics" from southern Europe, his parents settled in central California to live and work with their European countrymen. They were vineyard tenders and fruit growers. They led simple lives. They gathered in the same churches, attended the same festivities, spoke their mother language easily and affectionately. His father was a large affable man who worked in the large gathering sheds where crates were stacked along shaded walls waiting for the huge trucks to load and roll to the market. His mother, alone during the day, worried about Lionel and began early to fill him with fantasies of an adventurous life away from the vineyards, a life lived in the bosom of an imaginary America where glittering success was within reach of the gifted. Lionel grew into a sensitive adolescent, twitching nervously at the vague but now overblown fantasies that filled his head. In high school Lionel took the first steps toward finding a life away from the towns and villages clustered around the vineyards. Encouraged by his mother he changed his name to Lionel from the softer, though unpronounceable name given at his baptism. At a call for volunteer actors and theater hands at the leading community theater, Lionel discovered the arts. He chose stage design and set painting. He was challenged by the assignment of matching the mood of the play with visual effects he created. By the time he graduated from high school he had several plays to his credit and his reputation as a creative set designer was well established in his community. Encouraged again by his mother and moved intensely by his own fantasies, he shortly thereafter left the life of his parents and moved to New York where he enrolled for specialized courses in his chosen field of stage and set design.

Two years later in New York he met Marjorie at a little theater company. She was a fashion designer during the day and, like Lionel, volunteered her evening hours as wardrobe and costume designer with the theater group. Their work brought them together in their evening hours at the theater and often in their tiny flats, where they spent hours matching set to costume, talking colors and lights. Lionel was a worrier, easily frustrated and quickly defeated. When a director tactlessly dismissed a model that Lionel had submitted, only Marjorie would know his suffering. She spoke softly to him, assuring him that his model had more merit than the director could see at first glance. Her gentle encouragement would soon bring Lionel out of his despair, and shortly thereafter they were at work again side by side. In time they felt a deepening intimacy between them, though their talk and their behavior never ventured into the intimacy of lovers.

Inevitably a time arrived, a winter's night in Marjorie's flat, when the work had gone well and they sat back and talked easily of other things. The wine was warming and both nodded off to sleep sitting beside each other. Marjorie urged Lionel to sleep the night in her bed. Heavy with sleep, Lionel could only nod assent and fell quickly asleep lying beside Marjorie. She lay awake several moments studying Lionel as he slept, perplexed at the unceremonious ease he displayed in failing to turn to her as a lover. When they awoke in the morning, they drew close and held each other, exploring each other in random movements. Though Lionel felt sexual excitement rise in him, he also felt strangely restrained from carrying his excitement further. Marjorie boldly led his hand to her. He seemed willingly obedient, nothing more.

Thereafter Marjorie and Lionel found sleeping together comfortable and expected. In time their work together attained first success. Their partnership in a common craft drew them even closer together. Though their sexual activity never passed beyond the first night they slept together, they were content to satisfy their sexual urgings in random child play. Theirs was a compelling intimacy and, on the strength of its comfort and its silent permissiveness to hold each other away from mature adult sexuality, to no one's surprise, they were married. They rented a loft in an industrial building and, after weeks of remodeling, turned it into an attractive dwelling and workshop. It was the showplace of their social set.

They continued to live as the creative couple in their limited theater world. There were well-paid teaching assignments for both, special theater productions, some television work. They were doing well. Their friends regarded the couple as ideally suited. In a set where casual living together as free-thinking lovers was accepted, Marjorie's and Lionel's marriage pleased their friends all the more because it seemed carefully-planned and intelligently-based on deep common interests and matching personalities.

A year after his marriage, Lionel came upon his first adult sexual experience and with it discovered his sexual potency. His mate in this adventure was a bright, attractive, recently divorced student in one of his workshops. It seemed to have happened quite suddenly. She had casually asked him to join her at her apartment to judge several sketches she had done. Later in bed with the young woman, Lionel felt no restraint in consummating his sexual excitement. He felt joyous, almost grateful. Later that evening, in bed with Marjorie, he clung closely to her, as if in this embrace of Marjorie he might better understand what had happened hours earlier. He felt no sexual response in his closeness to Marjorie, only a warm reassuring comfort that he had succeeded at something, something he could not boast of to Marjorie. Yet he deeply felt that, if Marjorie knew, she would be as proud of him as he had felt earlier in bed with the young woman.

In the days that followed, Lionel seemed suddenly free. There were other sexual encounters, all of them successful, always followed by clinging closely to Marjorie as he lay beside her in their bed, finding silent approval in her responding softness. Lionel and Marjorie lay beside each other in their marriage bed ten years, and at the end of that decade they were virginal with each other. It was not long before reports and rumors of Lionel's sexual adventures became too widely known to ignore and Lionel and Marjorie quietly agreed to divorce.

Divorce from Marjorie seemed to endow Lionel with a quiet dignity. He continued in his life's work, seemingly free of any signs of emotional collapse which his friends fearfully expected. His work schedule remained the same. By agreement with Marjorie, he remained in the studio-loft while Marjorie took an apartment on the upper west side of Manhattan. When friends spoke to Lionel of his divorce, he responded quietly and seemed to be in some other world. He spoke of the unpredictability of life. He appeared removed in some philosophic mood that lent a suspicious tranquility to his character. When one spoke of Marjorie and their life together, he lauded her with a special touch of dignity in his voice. No, there was no resentment against Marjorie. Yes, he felt a sense of loss. What he perhaps could not know consciously was that Marjorie's leaving left him with the brief, transient sense of separation that a child might feel after moving from an old neighborhood into another. But they would be friends for life, he vowed.

Three years later he met Ellen. Younger by eighteen years, she was glamorous and uncommonly attractive. She was given to sudden enthusiasms and moved through Lionel's world of theater people, flitting like a restless humming bird, now here, now there. She seemed to be everywhere and she seemed unattainable; her restlessness seemed unbounded. For all of these things, and perhaps more, Lionel felt drawn to her. In her, he experienced a return of early fantasies of taming the unconquerable, of claiming her as his hard-won prize, and then with her under his spell, of draining her of her boundless restlessness. He courted Ellen, pacing her madcap ways, no matter where her sudden inspirations led them. They sat on the bank of the Hudson River far on the Upper West Side and threw pebbles in the river at midnight. They drove hours on end over parkways to lunch at a rural bistro in the Berkshires. Yet, even as he joined her in these adolescent frolics, he maintained a solemn tone in his endless warnings that she must quiet down and take her life and her future more seriously than she seemed to exhibit in her antics. When she wearied of his brief sermons on the value of settling down, she stood before him and locked her arms around his neck, rubbing noses with him affectionately, whispered, "Lionel, my lion, don't fence me in . . ."

Then once on a madcap weekend, filled with unplanned frivolities, they married. Two weeks later Lionel entertained once more in his studio-loft, this time with Ellen. Marriage, however, did not contain Ellen. He rarely smiled at her antics. Her only response to his scoldings was her decision to stay away afternoons and evenings. She arrived at the studio-loft very late in the evening or, on occasion, the next day at mid-morning. Lionel stormed, demanding that she act responsibly, take her marriage seriously, but Ellen made less and less effort to respond to Lionel's scoldings. She continued her own independent way. One night she did not return. The next morning Lionel found her brief note. She had gone off with Steve, a young actor, had left the city and would remain away indefinitely. Lionel was free to call a lawyer, if he wanted to. This was farewell.

It was then that Lionel fell into a deeply troubling depression. His loneliness was fierce. He spoke of nothing but Ellen's treachery and his own endless anguishing torment for not offering Ellen more understanding, for not joining her more freely. He blamed himself for driving her out of their marriage.

He turned to Marjorie who heard his tormenting complaints silently. Occasionally, she reminded Lionel of Ellen's youthfulness, but he appeared unaffected by hearing this. His thoughts and his talks with friends kept Ellen predominant, with one single theme: he had been harsh with her.

Friends encouraged him to date other women. Several friends arranged dinner meetings for Lionel, but none he met satisfied him. They were too old, too settled, too obviously intent on marrying; they lacked imagination. Lionel, past forty, balding and sagging at the belly, looked out at his world with the eyes of the young Lionel newly arrived from the vineyards of central California. He remained mindless of his age; he seemed fixated on youthful Ellens, madcaps, adolescent women. When he did find a young woman who resembled Ellen in manner and in enthusiasms, he was temporarily lifted. He went about singing her praises, saying how different she was from the others, and with predictable regularity each left him after the first wave of impulses had spent itself.

DONALD

We now turn to Donald, the second of our two male studies. Donald was an only child. He remembered his childhood as pleasant until his father turned to habitual gambling. In time his father became a compulsive gambler, often risking his weekly wages, sometimes pawning family jewelry. When Donald was barely eight years of age, his mother took Donald and fled her husband, explaining her behavior in a note that told of her unhappiness in her life with him. Several days later, Donald remembered, his father called for his wife and son to return to him, pledging that he was completely reformed. The little family then started a new life. They left the city and moved across the continent to California. Donald's father made good his pledge, in California his gambling ceased, and in time he became a man of unusual mildness. He spoke little, smiled little and appeared to go through his days at work and home cocooned behind a shell that kept him withdrawn from close contact with both his wife and his son. However strange this behavior may have appeared to his wife, it was a far more preferred version of her husband than the troublesome gambler of former years.

Donald's mother ruled over the household and took over the role of guide and inspirer to her son. A firm woman of un-equivocal views, she spoke to her son of his future with the plain certainty of an army captain outlining a military campaign. He would be a successful man; this was guaranteed to Donald in official tones. He would, of course, work hard; he would study hard, and he would find his reward for these habits as certainly as the sun rises in the morning. The adolescent Donald listened to his mother quietly and appeared to be in full agreement with her plans and predictions. Away from her, however, at school, he was a truant from his classes and he frequently moved from one mischief to another. When the school authorities discovered him at his pranks and confronted his parents with his mischief, there were the customary shocked scoldings and the expected penitent apologies. Donald barely managed to finish high school.

Following his service with the army, he faced what he has since described as a crisis he dared not feel. He was without plans or hopes. He felt impelled by a mounting anxiety to move in some definite direction, to make good on his mother's wishes for him. At a bar one afternoon a friend encouraged him to study accounting. The arguments seemed persuasive: it was an entrance into the world of business; it was a valued pro-fessional skill. Though that afternoon Donald scarcely knew the difference between an accountant and a mathematician, he leaped at the suggestion and quickly enrolled in accounting courses at a local college. He pursued his studies with com-pulsive energy. He studied without interest and often without comprehending. His attention wandered in his classes, his grades were poor, but he felt pressed to continue as if he were being driven by forces out of his control.

He dated easily in this period, and successfully, Donald reckoning success as an "easy score." Though several of his dates were bright and attractive, he failed to perceive them as whole persons. His dates were experiences that left him with little personal meaning. His women friends were objects that he used but with whom he could not share interior feelings. He acted in all respects like an "as if" character, one who moves through life without being in life. He spoke correctly and smiled appropriately. He conducted himself properly and performed in all customary ways, though he was entirely unaware, it seemed, that there might be more to give or that more might be expected.

One day he met Phyllis, a plain girl of good and solid family. Phyllis taught school in the elementary grades and took her work very seriously. She spoke glowingly of her feelings about her fourth-graders and, hearing her, Donald felt a secret envy at her absorption in her work. It was something he lacked, he knew. After several months with Phyllis he proposed marriage, largely as he explained to his friends, "because she knows what she wants, that girl."

After twelve years of marriage, long after Donald had completed his professional training and was securely launched as an accountant, after three children, and nearing the middle of his fortieth year of his life, he fell into despair. His work, his wife, his day-to-day routine began to pall until it became painfully difficult to rouse himself to a new day. Neither his work nor his wife offered him relief. On the contrary, the sight of his wife and the feel of his office deepened his despair.

It remained for long hours of counseling in his search for help to unfold his story. It was a story which, when pieced together, told of a life following orders issued by others: his mother, his friends, his wife. He had followed others obediently and, not until he had reached his fortieth year, had he found himself in a situation that felt alien to him. He asked aloud if others, his wife, his work, owed him something in return for his obedience, some sense of satisfaction in goals achieved, in a marriage and in an established family. When, where were the joys of goals achieved to come to him? Everything he had and had done now seemed dry to the taste.

He began to leave Phyllis and the children for days, then return, only to leave again. Perhaps these absences could have helped to give him a fresh perspective on things, but he used the absences as he used his time in high school. He played truant in an adult version of his earlier self. There were other women, transient, meaningless encounters, and then another return to Phyllis and the children. In time Phyllis, grieving futilely at his deepening despair, hearing, perhaps once too often, his frank truth that he felt nothing for her, encouraged him to separate and perhaps divorce. They were divorced within months following one such occasion when Donald reiterated his failure to feel any affection for her.

After his divorce Donald faced the most perplexing of all questions, a question which perhaps had to wait until after his divorce. *What did he really want out of his life?* He began to exhibit anger at his work and sometimes treated his clients curtly with ill-concealed contempt. His frequent but necessary phone and in-person conversations with his wife left him in a confused state of regret and annoyance. He found it difficult to reflect the insight that perhaps his work and his wife were not experiences of his choosing. It was even more difficult to explain to himself what it was that woke him to this impasse in his life. Depressing as these enigmas were, he evinced even more distress at the final question he asked again and again. Was he capable of making choices? Could he involve himself in experiences that could capture his will? Could he, in short, direct himself to a destiny of his choice?

SPECIAL PROBLEMS OF MEN AFTER DIVORCE

We return now to the question of how Lionel and Donald, two seemingly disparate personalities, perhaps atypical for our purposes, can illustrate the special problems of men after divorce. Were we to lay out major problem areas gathered from our two clinical portraits along one continuous spectrum, we might find significant clues to follow in our search to understand something of the special problems of men who enter the life of the divorced. One central problem that seemed to emerge following the end of Lionel's and Donald's marriages was the uncertainty of next steps.

Clearly the man, whose reasons for divorce existed in an extra-marital relationship, "the other woman" who managed to end the marriage, will not be plagued by the uncertainty of next steps. He brings no special problem to his divorce, for he appears to have stepped out of one marriage and into another, virtually by-passing the impact of divorce. But the Lionels and Donalds are not candidates for such certainties in life. Uncertainty has been an unseen but constant companion in their lives.

As Marjorie could not hold Lionel, neither could Phyllis hold Donald. Both men slipped away from their marriages. Both had married idealizations patterned by others. Neither had married personally felt choices. Both moved through their lives as self-perceived children who depended on others for guidance. In his divorce from Marjorie, Lionel abandoned his idealization but failed to replace it with another view of himself and his place in the world. Instead he fell back upon early but highly transient feelings that held the lure of excitement, of childhood dreams about to come true. He was drawn to Ellen and to all the later Ellens he met because they promised intense excitement, followed unhappily by the pains of frustration and exploded fantasies. It was only after his divorce from Ellen that Lionel came to sense, and yet feel compelled to enact again and again, his special problem playing the doomed moth drawn to the flame that could destroy him. For Lionel no problem, following his loss of Ellen, seemed more acute than his addiction to the alternating intensities of excitement and pain.

For Donald, life as a divorced man offered him the same problems he had known as a man all of his life. He could likewise no longer trust early idealizations, but perhaps, even more despairing, was his gnawing fear that neither could he trust himself to evolve a self-made view of himself with its hoped-for ability to know what was "right" for him.

Parenthetically, it seems clear that the task of the Counselor, in treating the special problem of divorce of his male client, must include a deeper knowledge of his client's total life, sufficient at least to arrive at an understanding of the sources of his client's ideas and idealizations. With this ongoing effort to understand the major influences in his early life, the Counselor is advised to involve his client actively in a critical review of his past in order that the client may himself grow to understand that ideas and values, once accepted by him as guide-lines to life, may have failed to bring him the satisfactions he had expected. It is at such junctures that the client should be helped to understand the lifelong need to so understand one's self that, when choices are made, they are felt as extensions of one's very self. Choices then cease to be autonomic behavior performed in unconscious obedience to earlier idealizations. The special problem of men after divorce is the task of mental house-cleaning. As in the Chinese symbols for Crisis, divorce flashes danger to the man who is compelled to repeat his mistake, the man who darkly senses that he is without choice.

The man who chooses to view his divorce as opportunity earns a long overdue breathing space between two time periods in his life. He will use the time for mental housecleaning and for serious examination of goals to pursue. He thus permits himself to move into new experiences without crippling preconceptions and without ulterior motives. He will in turn permit himself the freedom to reveal himself without guile.

The reader, who assumes that a critical discussion of the special problems of men in divorce must deal in depth and in detail with the customary areas of loneliness, sexual adventuring, separation from children, bachelor living and the host of stark realities that follow divorce, assumes the skills of meter reading to be prime requisites for the study of physics. The realities of sudden bachelorhood in its day to day problems in living are not problems in depth; they are transient hardships, painful and frustrating though they may be. Neither a "How to" discussion of where a divorced man may expect to find companionship nor an extended essay on the success/failure probabilities which he may expect to encounter in his sexual pursuits will bring understanding to the central problem as we perceive it.

The Lionels of this world will find emptiness wherever they turn, largely because they live with a sense of inner emptiness. One does not direct a Lionel to the fertile plains of new social opportunities principally because, without his conscious knowledge, he is obliged to defeat his advisors. He is, without awareness, bound to disappoint his advisors as he must disappoint himself. "How to" directions to the Lionels are doomed to fail. Lionel's very special problem is most sharply met through leading him to understand his own inner need to find triumph in defeat.

Men may differ in their ways of exploring their new life as divorced men. Some may enter that life vigorously, rushing to crowd appointment books with all manner of activity, while others may hang back passively for a time, fearful of testing the water. In either case, the aggressive and the passive man are both compelled to pause and look out upon their varied experiences, and each will be compelled to understand his life and his new experiences in far different terms than he had settled for in earlier times. Each will be beset by the endless question of knowing the "real" from the "unreal." He will inevitably sense that awaiting him is the responsibility to distinguish between a way of life that vainly leads outward to activity piled on activity, yielding little of the meaning he will need to guide him, and the long overdue search into himself. If he avoids the latter, the doors to meaningful experiences must remain closed to him.

It must be clear, therefore, that one of the tragic myths perpetuated in our society is the often heard notion that the most effective antidote to the loneliness of bachelorhood is instant activity. Activity and social opportunities can, of course, be palliative, but such a course exclusively pursued is as productive as gathering water in a sieve. Every man recently divorced must know the feeling at the close of his day that, though he conformed to the myth—he dated, he socialized, he was kept busy—the emptiness remained.

THE TRAGEDY OF MEN'S DUAL ROLES IN OUR SOCIETY

One may ask how the special problem of men stated here is essentially different from the problem of women after divorce. If the essential problem for men after divorce rises from a neglected need to understand one's self, to understand one's past, to understand past idealizations, to understand others' goals and values, it would appear that we have stated a universal problem, one that transcends in scope and depth the special situation of men. Certainly women know the emptiness of meaningless experiences as men do. Certainly women have been known to choose mates who were the illusory creatures of their early idealizations. How then do we claim this universalist problem as essentially a problem of men after divorce?

We make this claim on two main grounds!

1. In most instances, women after divorce continue to live in the same pattern as they did in their marriage. There are notable differences, of course, and these are of major consequence. The absence of husband and father is quickly felt within the broken rhythm of life in the home; there sometimes follows a cessation of an adult social life with other married couples. However major these differences may be, they exist at another level. The problem of divorce for a woman does not so much touch the deep inner center, the anxious feeling of personal failure. The woman's anxiety derives largely from a fear that she may fail at the task of continuing the pattern of homemaking and child-rearing alone.

The divorced woman is perforce preoccupied with survival problems. Imaginative, courageous women often find the period after divorce a rejuvenating opportunity to reenter the world of the salaried employed. They often learn new skills or brush up on old ones. They enroll for courses at nearby schools. Briefly, many women after divorce, following the first shock waves of separation, turn to a form of self-realization by taking on new roles as student or as worker. Divorce frequently leads to an emancipation of new roles that in time widen an earlier life made stifling by a failing marriage.

2. The male ego, influenced and shaped by a culture that sharply divides life's goals differently between the sexes, is burdened with a special set of expectations. However he perceives success in the specific terms of his ethnic, socio-economic class, the illusion of success for the male in our society transcends race and class lines. For many men, an unnamed desolation waits them after they find themselves relatively secure eco-

nomically; it is then they speak of a sense of loss, or emptiness, or disappointment, as though something promised long ago never entered their lives.

Life stories of men told in counselor's offices, theater dramas, movies, novels, all dwell upon the central theme of the emptiness in the lives of men. Tragedy strikes here with double force. At first, it brings a pervasive disappointment the feeling that something is lacking yet in their lives, something beyond economic security or even the appreciation of friends. The tragedy is accented by hints that the something which men vainly yearn after is elusive, its very form beyond human recognition. On these two main grounds, in the terribly special sense of man's fate in our society, divorce becomes a special problem of men. If his marriage was a promise and a pledge which he made to himself, if it was for him a special relationship in which he demonstrated qualities which have been lauded by untold generations, then divorce falls upon him as a shattering instance of personal failure.

Neither our folk culture, found in manners and customs nor our legal culture, represented in laws and court decrees, expect the divorced man to remain as head of the family which his marriage created. He is separated from house and home. He is removed from the life-flow rhythm he once lived in as husband and father. He is compelled to live elsewhere and he is spared the familiar preoccupations of keeping house and home together. Because of these extra consequences of divorce, his new and strange role of being without role leaves him confused and emptied. He may not take comfort from thoughts of entering new work, or learning new skils. Obviously, this opportunity does not draw him with the same necessity as it draws the divorced woman.

From still another perspective, men carry special problems because they are encouraged from childhood to suppress their feelings, least they appear weak before their peers. We shall elaborate on this perspective briefly. Three spheres of existence become increasingly articulated for all of us as we grow into life. Though each sphere calls for different roles and responses from us, we are obliged to perform in each sphere if we are to live full and vital lives.

First there are our families, the early one in the home of our parents and sibs, followed, after marriage, by the home we create and the family that grows from the marriage. A second sphere is our work life, school during childhood and young adult periods our lives, followed by employment in offices, factories, or the host of other settings. There is finally the third sphere, the larger world of friends, of organized groups, church membership, political parties. This is the world in which we express ourselves through our ideas, our ideologies. The latter world of friends and organized groups, important as it is to round out our existence, is for our immediate purposes not of primary significance. We are here principally concerned with a view of man as we observe him in the world of home and family and in the world of work. These are the two worlds in which man lives and functions continuously.

Each of these spheres requires different roles and responses, and each draws upon different levels and intensities of psychological functioning. In our families we experience ourselves and our "loved ones" primarily at an emotional level. Our relationships at home are unstructured, spontaneous and affectional. Here we lift restraints and live freely with all manner of expressions of feeling. If as children we cried and raged in our early families, we continue these basic feelings of anger and frustration in our later families, considerably transformed of course into some acceptable adult version. Home is the cathartic center for all of our feelings.

Away from home, at our work, relationships become structured, roles become defined, and our responses are more carefully drawn than at home. In brief, our work atmosphere, though often casual and warm, is rarely a replication of life at home. And for many people the overlay of behavioral restraint imposed by their work setting is felt as a welcome relief. Counselors and therapists are all familiar with men clients who suffer from "weekend" neurosis, a condition characterized by tension at home and an inability to relax at work. These men feel closer to some sense of inner comfort in the protected environment at work. Men in our culture are sometimes encouraged to idealize the work posture. In this posture the human qualities most valuable for success are antithetical to the qualities most desirable for life at home. The work posture becomes, not only an idealized image to pursue, but the norm, the standard by which male behavior is to be judged. In consequence, many men resist the free flowing rhythm of give and take, of the highs and lows in mood which characterize life within the bosom of the family. Many men confess to the difficulty of "shifting gears" when they reach home after their day at work. Some have solved the problem of the change-over in mood by asking for a brief time alone, away from the children, in a "decompression chamber" at home.

Yet in a study of six thousand men, aged 45 to 54, which sought to relate work success with marital success, it was found that those men who progressed furthest in their careers were still married to first wives. Next came the remarried, divorced, separated and widowed men trailed badly. For perhaps a special group of men who over-idealize the work posture, easy access to emotional expression appears to be shut off. These men describe scenes from their lives at home in which they stand mute and helpless as their wives pour out their rage at the now legendary "no communication." And sadly, perhaps, these men later justify their silence by characterizing their wives' behavior as childish. In time these men grow immune to angry demands for communication.

The idealized image of the successful man hence becomes a liability for many men. Admittedly, not all men in our work society are so addicted to the idealized image of the successful man. The marginally skilled laborer, the chronically unemployed, are likely burdened so early in life with the encompassing problems of poverty that at an early age their value systems are closely related to problems far more immediate than illusions of a distant success. Clearly the population we are dealing with is of men over 34 years of age, engaged in work pursuits that provide built-in potentials for advancement to positions of greater responsibility and more remuneration.

In the main, we have been observing men who appear to be psychologically split, condemned not only to having their emotional lives and their mental lives widely separated, but to having the mental life style, adopted for the work setting, threaten to eclipse the emotional life, draining it of passion and feeling. More than women, the man stands awkwardly above these two worlds of home and work. While he is at least accounted a full partner in his home in governing the affairs of his family, with immediate access to a position of power, at his work setting, he is often far removed from the center of power. When he thinks of power and its uses in the hands of the successful man, he envisions qualities and forms of human expression that are calculated to inspire others to emulate such traits. Thus he prizes silence and the visage of thoughtfulness. The outer hint of inner strength and stability is conveyed by a behavior of reserve. At home, however, these qualities could only earn him attack for standing at a distance and for being uncommunicative.

In large part, therefore, the special problem of men after divorce is suggested in the psychological ability to live comfortably in the two separate worlds of home and work, a phenomenon which our industrialized society has created for all of us. The casualties of this split may be seen in those men who are unable to shift gears as they pass from one sphere to the other. The traditional model of the autonomous family, classically structured in the hierarchy of father, mother, eldest son, daughters, working side by side in the fields in the shadow of home, has long since passed. Nevertheless it is that model which stubbornly hovers over us as the idealization of an entire society; it has by now become our folk mythology.

When a man can authentically *feel* his role of husband and father, he will function in these roles without difficulty. To reverse matters, to function in human roles without feelings appropriate to the role is to live imitatively. It may be a truism to say that divorce, as an event in the life of a man, bears the analogous significance of the sneeze to the cold; both are symptoms of a hidden problem. Though divorce may be a one-event experience in the total flow of life's experiences, it can also be a bottle-neck and seriously impede the free flow of other experiences unless attention is directed to it quickly.

Centuries ago men rose from apparent preoccupations with passions and condemned themselves for their failure to structure their universe. From Plato to Descartes, only the *mind* of man, its special capacity for reason was celebrated. Spinoza, himself the poet of reason, spent a bland life decrying man's bondage to passion. When this legacy touched our shores, our Puritan forebearers enshrined virtue as righteous behavior, and righteous behavior was measured in emotion-free behavior. The special problem of men today is made even more acute by the rapid emancipation of women, who no longer follow men's models of behavior. They are no longer passive and submissive before their husband's will. The danger may yet be that women, in their understandable struggle for emancipation, will read the new role behavior in sexual terms and hence choke off the sources of passion under a synthetic political fiat.

LaRochefoucauld once observed, "It is harder to hide feelings we have than to feign those we lack." This may well state the special burden which man has taken onto himself. The men we speak of here may have subordinated their behavior at home and thus emerged as partial persons, a too high price to pay for a view which regards behavior at home as trivial and inconsequential. "He who can take no interest in what is small will take false interest in what is great." This, perhaps is the tragic mistake of modern man, according to John Ruskin.

Chapter 4

SPECIAL COUNSELING PROBLEMS OF WOMEN

Helen Zusne

•••

INITIAL PROBLEMS

LETTING PEOPLE KNOW

COPING WITH AN EX-HUSBAND

COPING WITH CHANGE

RELATIONSHIP WITH MEN

FEELING OF IDENTITY

•••

ARE A WOMAN'S PROBLEMS of adjustment to divorce different from a man's? This depends on her age, background, habits, personality, the way in which she has viewed a wife's role in marriage, and her current attitude toward divorce. The ages of children, if any, and the number of children still at home contributes to the complexity of the situation. While many of the problems that a woman faces are like those of her former husband—problems related to loneliness, depression, anger, guilt, and shock—there are in addition certain problems unique to women, or at least occurring much more frequently in women than in men. The counselor needs to recognize that marriage does not have the same significance for men as for women. To a woman marriage is more important. She is more ego-involved in making her marriage work, and it is often her whole reason for existence. Therefore the impact of divorce is much greater on a woman than on a man.

In the following discussion it is not assumed that every woman faced with divorce is confronted with all the possible problems. To the extent that a woman is self-sufficient and independent in outlook and actions, her problems are less distinguishable from those of men. If she is a person with many interests outside her home, interests which she has not necessarily shared with her husband, or if she has been employed, has handled her own business affairs, or has shared in the handling of family finances, she will be in a better shape to cope with divorce. But if her entire life since her marriage has revolved around her husband and her children (or only the husband after the children have left); if she has cleaned the house only to please him, prepared only the foods that he liked, never the ones that she enjoyed; if her whole purpose in living has centered around him and she has little else in life that interests her; then the jolt of a divorce can be staggering. Her problems will be very different from those of her husband.

INITIAL PROBLEMS

During the time just after the decision to divorce has been made, and while the terms of the divorce settlement are being considered, your client will need a chance to ventilate her feelings and require considerable support, practical suggestions, and even direct advice. This initial period is especially difficult and frustrating for the wife because she is required to make important decisions at a time when she may not be in the proper frame of mind to do so. Her judgment is apt to be poor and her thinking foggy, although this is by no means always the case. The husband is one up on the wife at this time because he probably has had an opportunity to know more about the family's financial situation as well as business in general. The counselor does not need to give legal advice or play the part of a financial advisor, but he may need to call attention to some of the matters which need to be taken care of, but of which the wife is not aware. For instance, the wife needs to know something about the family income and budget and be able to make at least a gross estimate of how much she needs to support herself and any children who may be living with her according to her present standards or to just tolerable standards. It is surprising how many women do not know how much their husbands make a year, what insurance there is, or whether or not there is a savings account, investment program, or retirement plan. She needs help in choosing an attorney who will understand her needs and help her to decide what a fair and reasonable settlement would be.

At this time each woman needs to be protected from the harmful effects of her own particular emotional reaction, no matter what it may be. The counselor needs to be aware that, while some women react with bitterness and hate that turns to greed, others try to be noble, play the martyr role and rashly proclaim that they can get along with no property or support money at all. Few women can afford the luxury of telling their husband's, "I don't want anything from you, not one little penny."

Before she is confronted with papers to sign and even before she sees an attorney, the women needs to talk over with her counselor what her plans are concerning the couple's children. She will want to decide what she would prefer in the way of visitations. Later discord between the couple can be minimized if there are definite arrangements for visits from the parent who does not have custody, so that there will be no doubt or misunderstanding on the part of anyone. It may also save some worry about late support payments if arrangements can be made for the money to go through the court rather than to be paid directly to the wife. Some women who become temporarily unable to cope with their responsibilities toward their children because of the emotional shock they are experiencing, in desperation, allow the husband or grandparents to take over the custody of the children temporarily, only to regret their decision later when they attempt to regain custody. If the woman is experiencing severe emotional reaction, the counselor needs to take the steps necessary to prevent her from behaving in such a way that she may lose her children. Sometimes hospitalization is necessary.

After the divorce has legally taken place, there are aggravating circumstances confronting the new divorcée. It may even seem to her for a time that people are ready to kick her when she is down. For instance, in order to have a telephone in her name in the house where she may have lived for years, she must make a deposit required of new users; or, after having been employed and having paid for her own clothes and car for years, she now discovers that all credit was her husband's, and that she has no credit anywhere in town. She may have little experience with such matters as mortgages, transferring titles, paying utilities, income tax returns, car, health, and accident insurance.

LETTING PEOPLE KNOW

Many women suffer "untold" agonies before they are able to tell their friends, acquaintances, neighbors, family members, and their children's teachers that they have been divorced. This suffering is unnecessary, and the new divorcée needs to gain some understanding of her own attitudes about divorce in order to manage this hurdle. In general, it is best to inform others soon after the decision is firmly made and legal steps have been taken. Not only does this bring a feeling of relief, but children will feel less strain when the situation is handled in a frank, brief, and matter-of-fact way.

Usually it is the husband who packs up and moves out, leaving the wife in the old neighborhood with the task of explaining what has happened to friends and neighbors. The wife may, however, attempt to keep on in her old ways, hoping neighbors will not notice that her husband's car is around very little and at unusual times. She may pretend to herself, as well as others, that this awful thing is not really happening to her. To this extent she is not facing reality. Her attitude toward divorce may always have been inappropriately negative. Possibly she has been taught by family and church that divorce is "sinful." She may have been critical, in the past, and intolerant of her friends and acquaintances who have divorced and looked down upon them as failures or as being in some way inferior. Now she cannot bear to face the facts because to do so would require her to be critical of herself and to consider herself a failure. She may therefore use any defense she can muster to keep on as usual, throwing herself into various activities, keeping excessively busy, refusing to be aware of the change. The day comes, of course, when she must be aware of the facts and must handle her resulting depression.

Telling others about it can help her face the facts. If she cannot on her own muster enough courage, she will need the help of a counselor in handling intense feelings of humiliation and disgrace which stem from an unaccepting, intolerant attitude toward divorce and a feeling that she is somehow above such a thing. She may not believe that her friends and neighbors can be understanding until she gives them a chance. They can help her by their attitude to be more accepting of her situation and more tolerant of herself.

In counseling, rehearsal of what to say to neighbors when the opportunity arises may be helpful. It is not necessary to go into long explanations, to blame anyone, or to air one's anger or hate. Better alternatives are: "It has been a difficult winter. Jim and I are getting a divorce," or, "You probably have noticed that Jim hasn't been here much lately. We're getting a divorce." This is a time when many women need help in keeping their anger from spreading so that it appears directed at friends who have been uninvolved in the divorce. "How's John these days?" Mr. Peabody asks innocently of the recently divorced Melba. She lashes back at him with a sarcastic remark which leaves Mr. Peabody feeling as if John was surely wise to leave this horrible vixen. It is helpful to anticipate such questions and to discuss ways in which a defensive attitude is inappropriate and leads to unnecessary embarrassment, hurt, and perhaps loss of friends.

In the past the stigma of divorce has clung more to the woman than to the man, no matter what the precipitating circumstances. This is changing, at least to some extent. The old taboos against divorce are crumbling. A counselor can be of help here. Divorcée need not be a dirty word, and one need not act as if it were.

COPING WITH AN EX-HUSBAND

It is almost impossible for the relationship with a husband to be cut off instantly, cleanly, with complete lack of pain as soon as a divorce takes place. Business matters, division of property, and especially care of children and arrangements for visitations require some communication. Too much involvement with an ex-husband, however, is a risky business and puts both partners under constant strain. There are very few couples who are fortunate enough to go through a divorce and remain true friends, able to give advice and help to each other when needed while maintaining a casual, easygoing relationship. Such an ideal "divorce relationship" is something to hope for but not to expect, especially in the months and perhaps years immediately following a divorce. If one of the former partners must be constantly warding off hostile verbal attacks or feelings of guilt over the reactions of a former mate who cannot adjust to divorce, or if children are used as a means of continuing unsolved conflicts, then the chances for a friendly, casual, and relaxed relationship are indeed dim.

Overinvolvement with a former mate can be initiated by either the man or the woman, or both. Because women often tend to fit themselves into the role of a dependent, subject to the wishes of the head of the household, they have more difficulty than men in remaining independent when a former mate becomes aggressive in his efforts to reestablish contact.

Some couples experience the trauma of divorce repeatedly. Jan and Mark were married, then divorced two years later while students at a large university. Out of sense of guilt Mark kept reappearing to take out his tearful, depressed ex-wife, to be kind to her, to help atone for the hurt he felt he had caused her. Each time her hope was reestablished, only to be dashed again. For a while they would get along fairly well, but then the original conflicts loomed again. A period of time would then go by without Mark appearing, so Jan would look him up. They were unable to keep from seeing each other. Finally, not able to stand it any longer and close to a complete nervous breakdown, Jan left for a visit with relatives half a continent away. Soon Mark followed her, only to discover anew that he and his ex-wife could not get along. Now back at the university, he is attempting to apply himself to his studies and a job. But the cycle will repeat itself, for Jan also is planning to return.

Counselors can remind the client that she decided once that she could not make a go of it with her husband and that her decision was thoroughly considered. She needs to be encouraged to stick by her decision and to know that it is possible to get over loneliness and depression. If she gives herself a chance for readjustment and recovery she will eventually want to make new friends. To change her mind constantly or to allow him to change it and to keep plunging herself into painful situations over and over again can destroy her emotionally. By the time she takes legal action, or at least by the time the divorce is finalized, the women needs to have worked through her ambivalence and will know how to handle her tendencies to change her mind about divorce, or to swing back between love and hate.

Not only is it important for her to recognize and protect herself from her own tendency to vacillate about what she really feels about the man she has divorced, but it is also necessary to understand in what way her ex-husband's feelings affect his behavior. With such an understanding she can keep from being sucked into a situation where conflicts and inner turmoil become so intense that the pre-divorce problems seem mild in comparison. A newly divorced woman often needs assistance in coping with an ex-husband who comes around presenting problems. Ex-husbands come in various common varieties:

> 1. There is the ex-husband who refuses to consider himself divorced, at least where his wife is concerned. He may use as justification the idea that he is morally and spiritually married even though he is legally divorced. It seems to make little

difference to him who initiated the divorce proceedings. Such a man may drop in uninvited at any time of day or night, embarassing his ex-wife in front of guests, for instance. He may phone frequently with a minor excuse or none at all. He may consider what was once joint property as still belonging to him. He may even pick up and take with him a piece of property which was awarded his ex-wife in the settlement. He may ignore plans made concerning the children, and he may give them directions contrary to those given them by their mother while they are in her custody and even promise them outings which he knows their mother cannot approve of. He may descend like Santa Claus bringing expensive groceries his ex-wife cannot afford and expect to be invited to eat with the family at any time.

This kind of man may feel that he is still in authority and may give instructions or ultimatums to his ex-wife about how she should handle her personal affairs and conduct her business. Many a divorced woman is plagued by being constantly watched or followed as the ex-husband attempts to keep up with her comings and goings, especially if he hears that she is dating. He may even react with the righteous indignation of the married man whose wife is stepping out with another man. It is not at all unheard of for a former husband to expect to be treated with affection and to feel hurt when his ex-wife bristles and stiffens after his attempt to embrace or to kiss her. To react to such a man with anything but distance and coldness is to invite behavior on his part that makes him increasingly difficult to handle.

It appears that such a man wants all the advantages of being married as well as those of being single. He may use his knowledge of his former mate's dependency to wrangle his way back into the marriage, even though that may not really be what he wants. He may come to fix a leaky faucet, to repair the TV antenna, mow the lawn, even babysit. His former mate needs help to keep from returning to her old situation, unable to be free to let the old wounds heal or to start a new life.

Some men who accept divorce initially and allow their wives to adjust in peace for perhaps years, may suddenly come apart at the seams when they discover that their old discarded property has become valuable to another man. It is like an old coat—they don't want it until someone else appropriates it because of its warmth, wearing qualities, or good workmanship. If these men descend on their ex-wives who plan to remarry, they can cause a great amount of trouble at a crucial time when their former mates are trying to help the children to adjust to a stepfather.

A self-sufficient, immovable front, firmness, almost coldness, are necessary in order to cope with the man who cannot accept the reality of the divorce. His ex-wife often needs support to keep from showing compassion, for if she does he may try even harder to become involved again.

2. Then there is the ex-husband who has a need to complete unfinished business, who is compelled to continue arguments, to attempt to settle issues, to win verbal battles, or to perpetuate with his ex-wife the disturbed relationship which led to the divorce in the first place. Of course, it can be the wife who haunts her ex-mate in an effort to work through old grievances or to continue the disturbed relationship. She needs to recognize her urge to have it out "once and for all" with her ex-partner. With the help of a counselor she may be able to discipline herself and to avoid the temptation to start it all over again.

She needs to be aware when this is what *he* wants to do in order to keep from being drawn into a conversation about details of past misunderstandings. The counselor may go over with her the ways in which to avoid all unnecessary contacts and, at the same time, be courteous, businesslike and brief when encounters are necessary. The counselor will assist the client by letting her rehash these subjects in counseling sessions rather than with her ex-spouse. Some of the common rehash subjects which women are tempted to discuss with their ex-spouses are:

"If you had ever let me make one decision on my own . . ."

"If you had only taken me out to a movie, or dinner, or something at least once a month . . ."

"Nothing I ever did satisfied you. If you had ever given me one compliment . . ."

"You always cut me down . . ."

"You never appreciated how I worked for you and the children . . ."

"If you hadn't always sided with your mother . . ."

"If you'd just had the common courtesy to call when you were going to be late for dinner . . ."

"You never really did love me, did you?"

"Let me ask you just one question: why did you do what did?"

"All you ever thought about was yourself. You never cared what I wanted."

If the goal is adjustment to divorce, she must let the old cat die. One last nasty phone call, one more meeting to hash it all out, one more letter will keep old wounds from healing and will keep the client absorbed in past troubles to the extent that she cannot look forward to a new future.

3. There is still another kind of ex-husband with whom many women must cop. He is the one whose feelings of guilt are so intense that he must continually work at assigning blame for failure of the marriage to his ex-wife. His guilt may be directed toward either the events that occurred during the marriage or to the divorce itself. It seems to make little difference who first wanted the divorce. Such a man may be unable to keep from contacting his ex-wife in some way in order to throw the load of guilt in her lap.

The ex-wife needs to be wise to the game of tossing the blame load back and forth, so that she can stand her ground against maneuvers directed toward enticing her to play. Even though her first impulse may be to defend herself against unfair accusations and distorted "facts," she must realize that to do so will only make him try harder to blame her. Her ex-mate may need help in handling crippling guilt feelings, but all she can do is to assure him that she does not blame him, that both are responsible, and bring the conversation quickly to a close.

If your client understands some of the reasons for her ex-spouses's behavior she can save herself painful reactions to his tricks. It is as if his illogical feelings direct him to make her feel as miserable as he does by making her feel guilty so that he will feel less miserable. There are numerous ways in which a man can work at making his former wife feel guilty. He may preach and moralize using religious doctrines and Biblical quotations to back him up. He may put on the pathetic Peter act, presenting himself as sad, alone, depressed, with no one to fix his meals or wash his clothes, and with no money left in the bank—the innocent, hurt one. Of course, his depression can very well be genuine, but, if he goes out of his way to point out the tear drops on his letters to make sure his ex-wife knows he is suffering, there is probably a need on his part to make her feel guilty. Some divorced men continue this kind of behavior for the benefit of their ex-spouses even after remarrying and making an excellent recovery from divorce by any standard. The woman who has never seen her husband in tears, apologetic, humble, making declaration of intentions to change may be taken in by such behavior in her ex-husband and may actually feel that she is somehow completely responsible for his misery.

The unconscious need to project blame upon his ex-wife may push a man to treat her with unusual attention and apparent kindness which may mask for a while his feelings of hostility. It is difficult for her to react to kindness by being cold and ungrateful without also feeling guilty. It is not uncommon to hear declarations of intense love coupled with hostile critical remarks. So we have a man, who not once remembered an anniversary while he was married, sending flowers to his ex-wife on the anniversary of their marriage with a note: "You are a wonderful woman, and I would give the world to be married to you. I have never known anyone who could be so cold, deceitful, and mean."

Of all the difficult relationships with an ex-husband none are so painful as those pertaining to their children. Difficulties may revolve around misunderstanding or selfishness regarding arrangements for visitations, conflicts over discipline, or whatever else the mother sees in the behavior of her ex-husband which she considers as harmful to the children or as taking advantage of her. Often to defend herself makes the situation more difficult for her children. The husband may promise to come take the child on an outing and then never show up, and it is the mother who must comfort the waiting, disappointed child. He may shower the child with gifts, attentions, and excursions at one time, then neglect him for long periods; or perhaps he may give the child a longed-for bicycle which the child is then not allowed to take home. The father may subtly or openly berate his ex-wife in front of the children. He may use the children as a means of invading his ex-wife's privacy as he milks the childen about what is going on at home. The divorcée, who finds herself getting extremely angry over her husband's handling of the children needs a chance to ventilate her anger in counseling sessions and then to plan on a reasonable course of action which will not cause the situation to escalate.

Adjustment to divorce is never completely over. The years spent with one man leave their permanent effects, both good and bad. One morning Marge was sipping coffee at the breakfast table, across from John, her second husband, to whom she had been married seven years. She suddenly remembered something she wanted to tell him, and out of the blue came "Roger. . . ." She stopped short, clapping her hand over her mouth, realizing too late that she had called her first husband's name. The awkward silence, after a sheepish glance, was relieved with a "Pow" from John across the table. The old lament of the divorced, "all those wasted years," is not really so. The past is over, and what happens in the present or in the future cannot change it—or make good experiences of the past into bad experiences.

When the shock, the loneliness, and the bitterness and ambivalence have faded away, what can be considered the ideal attitude for a divorcée to have toward her former mate?

1. Understanding his behavior for what it really is in an unbiased, unemotional way.

2. Caring for him as an individual with his own problems, feelings, and right for happiness, an individual for whom she has concern and good wishes, but with whom she does not wish to be closely involved.

3. Refusing to repeat endlessly old conflicts or to be put in an intolerable situation by him.

4. Firmly insisting that living go on in the present, with an optimistic outlook toward a future which does not include marriage to an ex-husband.

5. Allowing memories of her past marriage to present themselves without dwelling on them or being caught up in intense emotions.

6. Regaining perspective and a sense of humor.

COPING WITH CHANGE

Drastic changes in life style often accompany a divorce. With women more often than with men these changes occur in almost every area of life and reach staggering proportions. Even to the women with personality traits of exceptional flexibility and resilience, such widespread changes coming simultaneously can be shocking and can bring on fatigue, depression, and anxiety.

It is not just the empty chair by the television set or the absence of men's shirts in the laundry. Nor is it even the quietness which comes with the absence of bickering, arguments, and accusations. A divorced man also has such adjustments to make. A whole new way of life often emerges. Thus we see a woman who has never held a job in her life attempting to earn a living, or a woman in her forties or fifties who has never pushed a lawn mower or done yard work exerting herself with sweat on her brow. Unless she is one of the few whose husbands were financially well off and she was able to get a generous divorce settlement, she will need to change her standard of living. Menu planning, meal preparation, and shopping habits may have to change radically. She may even have to buy clothes at different shops that carry cheaper brands. If she has children, she finds that, in addition to other changes, she has less time to spend with them. To hold down a job she must leave her children with a sitter or at a nursery. If her children are too old for that, she may have to leave them alone after school hours and worry about whether they are able to handle their new freedom wisely.

Perhaps after a day at an unaccustomed job she comes home with swollen feet and an aching back to find that her children have been uncooperative and have failed to do their assigned tasks. She may react with unusual irritability, only to experience endless repercussions as children react to mother's new demands and to her fatigue and irritability. It is no wonder that a percentage of women completely give up at this point. They are usually the ones with no experience of preparation for making a living, with a number of small children and very little support money, or with little confidence in themselves as individuals. Some of these women are forced back into an intolerable marriage or must give up custody of their children because they do not know how to handle the flood of new responsibilities with the resources available. Some of these tragedies could be avoided if the women would seek counseling and guidance at a community social agency or with a private psychologist or counselor, where they could learn to handle practical problems better and receive the necessary emotional support.

The initial shock of widespread change subsides as time passes. The picture is not all black for there are many positive results which accompany the upheavals. In spite of the probable shortage of money, time, and energy and the burden of responsibilities never before assumed, many women find their new life stimulating, challenging, even invigorating. The imprisoned housewife who has known only diapers and dishes now is forced to become involved with other people at her new job, and she feels more a part of the world outside the house. The pampered housewife who has been preoccupied with her own care may be forced to become a more useful and thus a more interesting person to herself as well as to others. The rigid, self-righteous woman has been roughly jolted from her smug and proper rut now is in a position to be more accepting and understanding of other people's problems, thus stretching her capacity for empathy with others.

When a newly divorced woman joins the ranks of the employed after a decade or more of unemployment, she experiences first hand the problems common to most employed women. Inequities and discrimination against women in the job market can be tolerated more easily by a woman whose marriage is stable and whose husband has an income which is more than adequate. Such a woman may be working for her own enjoyment or for frills, such as a summer vacation or a new swimming pool. Even the woman who has only herself to provide for has an easier time and is less bothered by inequities than the breadwinner of a family of seven people. Consider the new divorcée, as she is still smarting from unfair treatment she feels she received at the hands of one man, who tries to provide adequately for herself and her family. Even the most intelligent, ambitious, and capable of women may be in for a disillusioning experience that may leave her sour, not only toward her ex-husband, but toward men in general, and even toward a society that allows such prejudices and unfair practices toward working women to exist.

During early years of marriage when a woman is busy with domestic duties and is contented, even flattered, to be cared for by a man on whom she can lean, she may not be confronted with the problems of women's rights in the working world. The problem does not touch her then for she is enjoying her role and fitting in with the old traditional viewpoint of a woman's place being in the home. But after divorce, along with all the other changes, there is a new orientation toward herself and society, and she discovers that her ideas about women's place in the world have also changed.

George and Mary started dating steadily when they were both in the eleventh grade. George was an average student and he applied himself inconsistently to his studies. When he and Mary studied together his grades improved somewhat. She enjoyed school, was a brilliant student in a class of over four hundred. They were both eager to get married, but managed to wait until they were half-way through their sophomore year at the state university. Both sets of parents were opposed to the marriage, but George and Mary felt they could manage on their own, and they did. Mary dropped out of school and took a job at the University's Bursar's office where she worked full time until her husband had his Master's degree. The only interruption was a few months when their first child was born. They then moved to another city, and George was pleased with his first job and his income, which was much more, of course, than Mary's had been. He worked hard and during the years received several promotions. Meanwhile Mary enjoyed the luxury of being at home with her babies. As her children grew older and George was more than ever absorbed with his job, the responsibility for the children fell completely to her. She was active in Scouts and PTA and worked hard as a mother and housewife—but received no salary. George's work kept him out later and later as he found it necessary to meet his clients for dinner and drinks and to socialize in order to increase his sales. The marriage deteriorated as his drinking and her nagging increased and their positive involvement with each other faded away. The divorce settlement granted Mary a fine home, only partly paid for, and $100 monthly for support of each of three children who were not yet eighteen. At age 43, after not having worked for almost twenty years, Mary looked for a job. Although she was neat and young in appearance, she was turned down a number of times because she was too old or because she had not been working recently. Finally she found a job at $400 a month. She worked as a secretary for a young executive who came to depend on her for major decisions and much of the actual work involved in his job. With the child support, Mary had an income of $700 a month for herself and her three children (or four—until her 19-year-old daughter could support herself). Her ex-husband, on the other hand, had a balance of $1500 each month (after paying child support) with which to support himself and his new wife.

Mary was actually lucky when compared to the majority of divorced women who seek jobs after a long period of unemployment. She at least had some valuable, although not recent, work experience. She was neat-appearing, intelligent, and had some positive regard for herself as an individual. She could manage financially on what she received, but even with all this going for her she could not help but be acutely aware of the inequities which penalize working women at every turn. Her husband George was no more deserving, had worked no harder in his life, had even less potential than she when both were juniors in high school. Even if she had continued her education along with her husband, the chances are indeed slight that she could have been able to match him with respect to job responsibilities or salary. Thus one important change that many divorcées experience is a turn-about in attitude toward a woman's role in marriage and in the world of work.

No matter what the women's liberation movement may mean to an individual, or how ridiculous some of their extreme ideas may sound, at least it has made the general public aware of the unfair practices toward women which exist in employment. Improvements have been made, but there is still a long way to go before a qualified woman can be on equal grounds with a man in most job situations. Until then the new divorcée must cope with the situation which exists, hoping to find an area where discrimination is at a minimum and remembering that there are men who share her viewpoint. She must console herself by telling herself (provided basic needs and requirements are met) that the amount of income does not measure happiness, feelings of self-worth, or individual freedom.

The divorced woman whose children are grown has problems which are somewhat different. If she is employed, the change in her life which may bother her most is dealing with the quietness of a house when she comes home from work.

Many women, who come for counseling after a divorce, report that they can cope well in the daytime but are tormented by the empty house in the evening. They try a poodle with a noisy collar, an unwatched TV turned to a high volume, or moving out of the house to an apartment complex where walls are thin and noises abound. The mature woman who has never been employed and who has already suffered depression and a feeling of uselessness when her children left home for college or homes of their own, now has problems which are actually agonizing. Her children no longer need her, and neither does the man to whom she was married for perhaps most of her life. Such an individual must start from scratch to find new, useful activities, new friends, and people to help, all of which can keep her from turning her attention inward, toward herself. With professional help she may discover a new purpose in life.

A young woman without children should have an easier time handling changes brought about by divorce, because her patterns of behavior are not as deeply ingrained. It should be easier for her to consider her marriage that has just ended a valuable experience which has helped her learn more about herself and the nature of intimate relationships. She may even wish to change back to her maiden name. It is not necessary to use the title "Mrs." and advertise to everyone who notices the absence of a husband that she has once been married.

Some women can tolerate more change than others. They may decide that, while they are changing from the married to the unmarried state, they will also make a number of other major changes which are not compulsory. It is not unheard of for a woman to get away completely from the old setting—a new town, new state, new job—and make a fresh start. Whether to undertake such a radical change depends on some practical considerations. Are there friends and relatives nearby? Can the new divorcée tolerate loneliness until she can make friends? Is the move economically feasible? Will there be a tendency to cling in an unhealthy way to grown children in the vicinity? Is the move motivated merely by a desire to escape the imagined or real reactions of friends and relatives of the divorcée? If the change is a running back to a childhood home with mother and dad, it will probably not be one which will facilitate a healthy adjustment to divorce.

Excessive change is a shock and strain even when conditions improve with change. Changes that accompany divorce are usually more extensive and complex for women than for men. It is a wise woman who seeks professional help during this difficult period.

RELATIONSHIP WITH MEN

A satisfactory adjustment to divorce has not been achieved until your client is free to establish mutually satisfying relationships with men, whether these are intimate, long-term relationships or casual everyday encounters. Let us consider some of the difficulties in relating with the man just divorced. The following ways of reacting are some with which the marriage counselor will become familiar.

1. Bitterness. Mabel Fry treats all men in an impersonal, cold, and distant way. Any man who has occasion to have conversation with her feels her unspoken hostility, and transacts his business quickly to make an exit. She perceives all men as selfish animals who have designs on her as a possible handy receptacle for their semen.

2. Live it up. Lucille Fling overreacts to her freedom. Although for years she has been ultraproper, she now embraces poorly considered experiences with any man available. She feels she has missed something and now she is hunting desperately for it in the most unlikely places.

3. Fear of rejection. Molly Small longs for and needs a relationship with a man, but she is unable to allow herself to be really close to anyone for fear she will be hurt again.

4. Ten down and hundreds to go. What better way can Sandie Bell express her hatred for men than by loving and leaving them. The more notches in her chastity belt the better. Although she believes that she loves all men, it gives her an unconscious delight to be seductive, make them fall for her, and then hurt them as she has been hurt.

5. So sweet to compete. Harriet Smith felt inferior to and belittled by the man she was once married to. Now she attempts to zoom ahead as an aggressive, industrious, efficient, and ambitious woman, rebelling, proving her worth, competing fiercely.

While her reaction may result in worthwhile accomplishments, it will not help her to establish a stable relationship with men.

6. Propping up a sagging ego. Her husband never seemed to care, so little wonder that Janice Redman felt like a real woman when she found out that there existed a man who enjoyed making love to her. So she tried it again with another man, and again, and again. . . Oddly enough, no matter how often she propped up her ego, when morning came it had sagged again. She could never form a real relationship, because she was concentrating on quantity rather than quality in her relationships with men.

7. Daddy, help poor little me. Darlene Clingon has an air of innocence about her that the boys fall for, and she uses it to get job promotions, attention, and extra favors from neighbors who mow her lawn and help her fix her car. She gives them a sweet smile and lowers her curly lashes over her big brown eyes. And that's it! She has never had the capacity for a mature relationship with a man, but she enjoys the admiration and attention which her dependent manner evokes.

The divorcée's relationship with men is complicated by the way men regard a divorcée. Many men think that the divorced woman is a sex-starved hot mama ready to jump into bed with any man who crooks his little finger. The divorced woman who finds a job as a secretary often has more than her share of problems in handling the boss who feels he has the right to handle her wherever and whenever he chooses. A number of recently divorced women are forced to give up badly needed jobs because they do not know how to resist advances on the part of their bosses without offending them. They may need help to learn how to respond in an easy, light manner, using some flattery to build up the boss's ego while giving a firm "no" which may get the message across to him without causing him to be angry.

Many men do not understand the nature of a woman's sexual needs, which they feel are as immediately pressing and urgent as their own. Your client may not understand how to cope with such men without increasing her bitterness and resentment which prevent her from having a reasonable relationship with any male. Clients report incidents in which the husband of a best friend or a neighbor they have known and trusted for years calls around to offer his help in satisfying the sexual needs of the recently divorced woman. If she reacts to what the man feels is a generous offer by becoming angry, he may feel that she really has a problem and is indeed a prude. It is a common complaint that, if a divorcée accepts a date, her escort assumes that she will want to go to bed with him as, of course, some women do. At this point many divorcées become soured on all men and decide to eke out a lonely existence without them.

Denial of sexual needs is not the best solution for the divorced woman. How she handles her needs depends on many factors: how capable she is of attracting men; what are her neurotic reactions to men; what are her moral and religious convictions; what are her underlying attitudes toward sex and to what extent can she accept her own sexual needs; how rigid is her personality structure; and what her ability to compromise is in the handling of conflicts.

Sublimation, or the draining off of sexual energy by engaging wholeheartedly in a constructive activity, is a workable emergency measure for a few women who are athletically talented or are creative individuals who paint, compose, or write. The day arrives, however, when sublimation is not enough.

Mechanical means can be used by some women to relieve specific and recognized tensions which are sexual in nature. Many women, however, are shocked, offended, and repulsed by the idea of masturbation. In counseling with such women the subject must be approached in an indirect, descriptive way rather than offered as an idea that the divorcée can use. Attitudes change slowly, and advice given to a woman before she can accept it will be useless. Masturbation is a substitute measure, at best, which fails to offer the warmth, understanding, and feeling of belonging that must accompany the sex act to make it a satisfying experience to most women.

Sex with just any male is not the right solution for the majority of women. What many men fail to understand is that for most women the act of sex itself is not satisfying, regardless of the occurrence of an orgasm, unless the woman feels that there exists between the two people a genuine emotional involvement with a feeling of commitment, some degree of permanence in the relationship, mutual respect, and empathy for each other.

The woman with rigid ideas of right and wrong finds that her need for intimate involvement with men clashes with her need to follow a strict, unbending code of ethics. It takes time and patience on the part of both client and counselor for such a woman to gain insight and to become understanding and accepting of her own conflicting needs. Finding a workable solution for such a woman is not simply a matter of brief counseling with respect to sexual behavior as such, but rather requires ongoing therapy for a considerable length of time, with the focus upon changing attitudes and outlook as she gradually gains tolerance of herself and others in a similar situation.

FEELING OF IDENTITY

Helping the newly divorced woman regain her sense of identity is one of the most important goals a counselor can have for his client. Too often married women lose their own identity as they lose their names. So Martha Crawford becomes Mrs. Harold Rothchild, wife of the new school superintendent. (Who ever heard of Mr. Martha Crawford?) When Ginny Krietmeyer married, she vanished, and in her place there was "Tom Duggan's pretty little wife" or "the druggist's wife." It is sad that marriage causes so many women to become mere shadows or extensions of their husbands, known because of what their husbands are or what their husbands do or have. When the Duggans divorce, what happens to Tom Duggan's shadow? Who is she? She must establish her own feeling of identity, which is built around her own view of herself as a person, the view others have of her, and the feedback she receives from them. She needs to become known for what *she* is and what *she* does. At first she may not quite know. Ginny Duggan was redecorating her living room and discovered in counseling that she was, out of habit, choosing the type of furnishings she knew her ex-husband would have liked instead of the kind that she had almost forgotten she really wanted. Self-esteem, confidence in her ability to make decisions (even though they may turn out to be mistakes), and pride in her own individuality are part of the feeling of identity, which can be a fortunate by-product of divorce, that will help the divorcée in future adjustment whether she remains single or eventually remarries.

Chapter 5

COUNSELING NEEDS OF THE CHILD OF DIVORCE

Marjorie Kawin Toomim*

●●

WHAT IS LOST?

THE MOURNING PROCESS

HOW DOES THE CHILD DEFEND AGAINST LOSS?

HOW CAN THE PARENT DEAL WITH THE CHILD'S DEFENSE BEHAVIOR?

REFERENCES

●●

T HE CHILD of divorcing parents must cope with a multitude of losses. While on the surface it appears that he has lost only the easy availability of a parent, in fact he has lost much more. He has lost a basic psycho-social support system. His own dynamic structure has been molded by this system; the fibers of his being have been interwoven with those of his family members in a way which, if not altogether positive for growth, were at least familiar and in some sort of balance.

---

* The author wishes to thank Lillian Freeman and Pamela Kawin for their assistance in the preparation of this paper.

With the dissolution of the structure, the child must now find new support systems.

The process of coping with loss is the same, whether the loss is of a person, a relationship, or a possession; whether the cause of loss is death, divorce, or a marked widening of psychosocial distance (Bowlby, 1961). Losses must be mourned in order to satisfactorily separate from a person or relationship and to allow new persons and relationships to fulfill one's needs.

How the child copes with the loss and the mourning process is crucial to his future development. A certain level of ego-strength, psychic energy, and external support is necessary to carry the mourning process through to completion. Few children have the capacity for healthy mourning before the age of three and a half to four years (Siggin, 1961). Few children of divorcing parents have the requisite external support at any age.

In divorce, the problem of accepting loss and properly mourning is complicated by the difficulty of discriminating the exact nature of the various losses. Even when the father deserts, his loss is not clear and the child may feel justified in hoping for his return, though, in fact, there is no hope.

Divorce losses are difficult to discriminate. Parents compound the problem by ignoring or denying that such losses exist. Some parents are too absorbed in their own pain to help the child appropriately; some do not recognize the various losses, naively believing that only the person of the father is gone. Parents may even state that the child has not lost his father at all, or claim they will now have a better relationship because they will see more of each other. Where such denial of reality of loss occurs, the parent and the child cannot share mutual thoughts and feelings or explore alternative ways of meeting needs together. The gap grows wider and losses mount. Parental failure to help in this trying time also alienates the child from himself. The child cannot cope with the overwhelming nature of his feelings. He defends against them. He denies, represses, withdraws, regresses, projects, detaches. He retains in fantasy what is not there in reality and he does not adequately deal with the loss.

Incomplete mourning leaves a reservoir of painful memories and feelings experienced as an undercurrent of depression. A rigid defense system guards against the awareness of ambivalence and pain and is a distorting screen through which subsequent realities are passed, misperceived, and misconstrued. The pain of the loss remains buried, occasionally surfacing when defenses are lowered or "reminders" of the loss transcend the defense barrier. Energy must constantly be expended to hide the pain. Distortion of reality creates difficulties in living; avoidance of stimuli which might bring the pain to the surface leads to a narrowing of life-space. Loss follows loss as the individual finds himself only partially alive, unable to partake of whole areas of existence. Energies bound in denying and avoiding the reality of loss and its associated pain are not available for use in positive growth and development.

Loss hurts; it leaves scars; it diverts one's life-course. Acceptance of loss provides freedom to explore other alternatives in life and to have other experiences. Denial of loss leaves a gaping hole that may only be covered over. There is constant fear of falling into the darkness below. Denial of loss leaves a vacuum in which no substitute relationship can flourish. Needs are left unsatisfied. The feeling of loss pervades one's life. Acceptance of loss and healthy, complete mourning provide a stable base for future growth.

Some of the trauma of divorce can be prevented by advance planning. Divorcing parents prepare themselves by a long period of questioning, expressing feelings, protesting and despairing, exploring alternatives in fantasy or in fact. Much of their mourning process is experienced in the context of the marriage. The child, on the other hand, is not prepared for this major change in his life. Furthermore, he must adjust to sudden loss in a chaotic family setting.

Parents need to respect the ways in which the child copes with divorce. His stress is great, his capacities limited. He does what he can to protect himself from what might be overwhelming stress. The parent may guide his adjustment patterns with tenderness and love, not with criticism and anger. The divorce adjustment takes years, during which time the dynamics need to be worked through repeatedly as the child's emotional strength and conceptual abilities mature. Young children almost universally deny some aspects of their situation. The aware parent can help the child integrate the realities the child brings to awareness as his strength grows. Insistence that the child see the whole reality at once will only bring resistance and move him futher into denial and fantasy.

The following sections on "What is lost," "The mourning process," and "How the child defends against loss," describe in detail the complexities of divorce from the child's point of view. They are written to alert parents and counselors to interactions which often occur for children of divorce. With this knowledge and parental self-awareness, the strain of divorce can be minimized. A good divorced family structure may even allow for growth not possible to attain in the failing marriage. They are not intended to deter parents from divorcing, only to help them enter into this new family relationship intelligently and with care. Divorce may be the most important event in your child's life.

WHAT IS LOST?

1. Loss of Faith and Trust.

A tacit contract is entered into by parents upon the birth of a child. The parents, in effect, promise to establish a firm psycho-social base from which the child can grow. In return, he is expected to remain with the parents, to develop and mature. The child in a two-parent family generally expects that the parental unit will continue to be available to him until he no longer needs it. Most parents encourage this belief by assuring the child of their love, concern, and intention to maintain the family structure. Most parents, experiencing a strain in their relationship, are especially vocal in such reassurance hoping to allay his fears and "make him feel secure." They do not want him to be unnecessarily upset, just in case they are able to remain together.

For the child, it does not matter how unhappy the parents are together or how reasonable and right that they separate. He only sees that they have been unable to solve their problems in such a way as to maintain *his* security. Even where a parent is cruel or the strain in the relationship so great that divorce would ultimately benefit him, the child has no assurance that his lot will improve. He feels betrayed. He may feel so hurt that he never trusts again. The younger the child, the less he can understand, the more his need for both parents, and the more his need for a stable family unit, the more divorce will leave him feeling betrayed, angry, hurt, and untrusting.

The hurt, untrusting child is in the uncomfortable position of needing help from parents who have just betrayed his trust. The likelihood of finding someone outside of the family to help him through this difficult time varies with the age of the child and his level of socialization. Very few children under six years of age have this ability. Beyond six, the willingness to ask for and receive help, the willingness of the parents to allow him to form a closer relationship with another adult or good friend, and the availability of a suitable, supportive individual are crucial factors.

Many children at this point deny their dependency needs and withdraw rather than trust either a parent or a parent-substitute. Or they may remain aware of unfulfilled dependency needs and feel helplessly angry. The child who remains aware of dependency needs and refuses to trust places himself in the precarious interpersonal situation of feeling unsatisfied and of being unsatisfiable. He has laid the grounds within himself of a double-binding situation that may persist into adulthood where he simultaneously demands and rejects love. As a result, his needs remain unmet and he remains frustrated.

Parents are generally advised (Despert, 1962) not to distress their child unnecessarily by telling him of their difficulties before they separate just in case things can be "patched up." My experience with family crisis is that the child is aware of conflict but does not understand it. Mistrust grows in such an interpersonal setting. Parental honesty builds trust. Parents can be open about the seriousness of their difficulty without burdening the child with unnecessary details, fighting in his presence, or using him in their struggle. Rather, they can *talk about* the fact that they have problems and how they are trying to solve them. The child usually can understand the parents' situation if it is discussed in terms of the child's own difficulties with playmates. Care *must* be taken to understand the extent of his ability to deal with the details of the conflict.

The separation counseling model provides an optimum situation in which the child can be prepared for divorce. Such an approach not only builds trust, but also provides the child with an effective model for conflict resolution. Even the concept that separation may be a constructive step in problem solving may help the child. Knowing when to end a relationship is a sign of strength and success, not of failure.

Maintaining open communication between parent and child helps to build his trust and provides a strong support for him. Only thus can the parents help the child cope with the many changes with which he will be faced as he grows in a divorced family. It is important that parents understand the child's experience of divorce, the logical and moral systems under which he operates at various developmental stages, and the ways in which this particular child copes with stress. Without this understanding the parent runs a high risk of being misunderstood and rejected.

Respect for the child's attempts to cope with his difficulties will also increase parental availability and support. The child who feels accepted will be more likely to keep the parent informed of how he perceives the changes in his life and will ask for continued clarification of his thoughts and feelings. As the child develops, he is increasingly capable of conceptualizing and integrating the whole reality of divorce.

2. Loss of the Child-Mother-Father Relationship.

In an intact family, the child has a child-mother relationship, a child-father relationship, and a child-parents relationship. Each parent gives him something; each provides a measure of support, control, nurturance, etc. Together they compliment and supplement each other. Even parents in conflict represent a unit. In fact, they represent a very strong unit if, for example, the child has learned to use one as a rescuer when he displeases the other, or if he has learned to gratify his needs by using their divergence to manipulate.

Unless he has assumed a large portion of child-care functions, the father of the infant from birth to eighteen months is more important for his role than for his person. The infant is primarily involved at the interpersonal level with his mother, especially in executing the difficult task of breaking his symbiotic bond with her and establishing his individuality (Mahler, 1971, McDevitt and Settlage, 1971). The father now represents a vital source of support for the mother, permitting her to give the child consistent care so that he may gradually learn to cope with separation according to his daily needs and capacity to tolerate stress. The father also represents a safe person the child can go to as he explores nonmother space. Relating to both father and mother gives him social skills necessary for complex interpersonal relationships. After the child can hold images of absent people and objects in his mind (18 months or before), the loss of the father as an *individual* is increasingly important. Also, he grows more vulnerable to even brief separation from familiar people, places and things. Until he can maintain a sense of self when separated from his parents, especially his mother, he is particularly likely to be hurt by divorce. At least three years of stable mother-child relationship are required to complete the separation-individuation process successfully. Oedipal experiences of the three- to five-year-old are difficult to work through in a disrupted family, and nonparental friends and lovers intensify the Oedipal crisis.

The child whose parents stay together during the vital period in which basic identification patterns are established will gain ego-strength. Even though parents differ markedly, the child is better able to take from each in an integrated way when they are together. It is also easier to talk about these differences with parents while they are together. Divorced parents seldom are able to talk about each other with good feeling, particularly when value and life-style differences are involved. As parents separate, differences tend to become accentuated and criticized. What the child perceives of his parents is then filtered through this screen of negativity. A parent may be so anxious to pass his value systems on to a child and mitigate the values of the other parent that he pushes too hard. Such an approach leaves the child confused and likely to reject the values of *both* parents.

The older the child, the less the difference between the parental value systems, and the greater the parents' ability to treat each other with respect after divorce, the less serious will be the loss of the parental unit for the child. Maintenance of open communication between the parents minimizes the loss of the parent-unit for the child. As stepparents are added to the child's extended family, such open communication greatly aids his ability to integrate new relationships, with their attendant value systems and changes in control and dependency patterns.

3. Loss of the Pre-Divorce Mother.

It is generally the custom for children of divorce to remain in their mother's custody. Therefore, I am going to conceptualize the child's changing relationship with his mother in these terms.

The divorcing mother is in the process of changing her life. She must cope with her own feelings of loss and anxiety. She must find alternative ways of satisfying the needs formerly met by her marriage. She may have to find or change work. She may begin to look for other interpersonal relationships. She probably needs to lower her socio-economic level, which means she may become less giving of things that cost money while, simultaneously, she is giving less of her time and attention. The child then feels rejected. Conversely, a divorcing mother may change her relationship with her child by turning to him for need-gratification. She may begin to spend too much time with him, to use him for her emotional support. This child feels smothered.

Many mothers at this time become quite inconsistent. Some quickly try to be "both mother and father," precipitously changing nurturance and control patterns rather than waiting for a new interpersonal balance to evolve. The mother, concerned with her own adjustment, is less available and less sensitive to the child, leaving him with more cause and opportunity to break rules. At the same time that she provides this latitude, the mother may be more punitive or harsh when she does realize that her limits have been violated. Or she may be more harsh because she must deal with control issues when she is over-burdened by her own problems. She may then react to her own punitiveness by guilt and overconcern. She may become over-permissive and allow too much freedom because she feels guilty about the divorce or feels this kind of giving will make up for the child's loss. She may be just too overwhelmed by her own adjustment problems to expend her energies in child-control. That is something she can "always do later." Perhaps the school, or a "Big Brother," or the "father-when-he-comes-over" will do it for her. She may use her energy to get a new husband-father who will assume the child-control function for her. Sulla Wolff, (1969) discussing children of deceased fathers, notes that adjustment was better when their homes were kept intact by mothers who were independent, hard-working, and energetic and who took on the working role with little conflict. Qualities of warmth and affection, deemed of primary value for the married mother, are less important for the separated mother. Mothers who clung to their children for support, especially their sons, impeded their maturation. Sons of such mothers tended to be tied to the mother and had difficulty establishing a good sexual adjustment.

Personal qualities of mothers may change a great deal as a result of divorce. Some mothers feel relieved at the resolution of their marital conflicts and thus are more relaxed with their children. However, if they become heavily involved in dating during this euphoric period, their children feel deprived and rejected. Mothers who feel depressed and overburdened by the stress of divorce, though they stay home, are experienced as rejecting by their children. However the mother responds to divorce, the ways in which the child has learned to cope with her are no longer altogether satisfactory. Some change must be effected in order to function well with her again. In addition, the post-divorce child has different needs and so requires new maternal qualities and behaviors. Thus, pre-divorce reciprocal-role relationships are lost, and post-divorce relationships must be established.

Children tend to idealize the pre-divorce mother, may try to cling to the fantasy that somehow they can get her to change back to her "old self." Feelings of guilt, inadequacy, frustration, and anger arise when they cannot. At times, they believe that the return of the pre-divorce mother will bring the father back. These manipulations of the post-divorce child serve only to create greater stress for the post-divorce mother. She thus becomes even more "different" than she was. The clinging child is further alienated.

A mother who is fairly stable emotionally, has a firm sense of values, and has established pre-divorce support systems for herself, in addition to those provided by her husband and the marriage relationship, is less likely to change much within herself after divorce. She will, as a result, be more accessible to adapt to her child's changing needs.

If the father cannot provide for the family's support, the mother should establish a work pattern and child-care facilities before separation. Thus, her stress is reduced at the time of divorce and the child is given an opportunity to cope with this change within the frame of an intact family. The mother who is unable to cope with the changes in her life comfortably should seek counseling. She thus minimizes the loss of the pre-divorce child-mother relationship.

4. Loss of the Pre-Divorce Father.

In a divorce in which the father leaves the home, the father-child relationship changes drastically and precipitously. In the ordinary family, the father works regularly, and thus is available to the child in a more limited and structured way than is the mother. After divorce, the structure becomes more rigid and highly limited in time and space. Thoughts and feelings the child may wish to communicate to the father or the sharing of activities must wait until the appointed time. And at that time, both the psychological and the physical space in which father and child meet are often not conducive to the delayed communication or activity. Maintaining a flowing, comfortable, in-depth relationship is ordinarily difficult for many fathers and their children; it is almost impossible under divorce conditions. Time with father is often time to be close "whether you feel like it or not." The closeness, if achieved, must be broken off at the appointed time or "Mommy will be mad" or "because Daddy has other plans for the evening." Many children will not open themselves to closeness under these conditions. Many will not tolerate the pain of repeated separation and loss. It is like reliving the divorce with each contact. Many children are fussy and angry with their mothers after a happy day with father.

Ongoing reciprocal role-relationships between father and child are disrupted in the event of divorce where father leaves the home. The only roles that are traditionally given to the absent father are those of financial supporter, the giver of fun-times and extra goodies, and the person who leads the child to much of the outside world through trips, talk of work or business, etc. If the father has held the traditional role of disciplinarian, he cannot do this well at the end of the week or over the phone. Also, he may be reluctant to discipline the child on his visiting day for fear of leaving the child with a bad feeling about him.

In the pre-divorce family with an active father, his authoritarian role contributes enormously to the ethical-moral value structure of the home. If the father has held the role of rescuer in mother-child struggles, his help will now be rejected by the mother as interference and side-taking unless she actually solicits it. The child may have difficulty accepting the father's help because of mixed feelings and divided loyalties. He may even use such help against the mother or accuse his father of trying to take him from the mother.

The father's role as provider of the masculine principle in the child's life is difficult to maintain on a limited contact. Visiting the child or going out to "have fun" can not replace the feeling that exists when a father actively lives in the home. This feeling is one of almost magical strength and protection against evil or powerful forces. It often transfers from the man to the child, even though by adult standards he might be considered weak and ineffectual. The concept of father as strong protector is further threatened by maternal criticism of the father. Also, the fact that the father does not return or is prevented by the mother from returning home and thus putting the child's world "right" again may be evidence to the child that he does not have the power to help at this important juncture in his life.

Biller's (1971) review of research studies of father-absent sons indicates that the loss of the father as a sex-role model has more effect on boys before the age of six than after. Father-absent boys tend to be less aggressive and less interested in sex-role stereotyped activities than are boys whose father remained in the home. However, the effects of father-absence on sex-role stereotyping may be mitigated by the mother's positive attitude toward the absent father and other males, and by her generally encouraging her boy's masculine behavior. Father-absence does not significantly affect the sex-role stereotyping of girls.

The continued availability of the post-divorce father in part determines how much is lost. However, the child's fantasy relationship with the father may be more significant than his actual presence. For example, an adolescent girl of sixteen had maintained constant contact with her father through wish-fulfilling daydreams and fantasies since his desertion in her third year. The fantasies were reinforced by his monthly support check, one letter, and one gift a year and her mother's constant complaints about him. On the other hand, a twelve year old girl, whose parents divorced when she was four and a half, often refused to respond to his daily telephone calls and went with him Sundays only reluctantly at the mother's urging.

Father-absence in divorce is ambiguous. Unless he has deserted totally, he is clearly available to the child at some times. Children believe their fathers could make contact by phone, or could come "if they really wanted to," or loved the child enough, etc. The post-divorce father is there but not there. Such a frustrating situation predisposes the child to respond with father-idealization and clinging or with resentful rejection.

Any action that minimizes the ambiguity of the post-divorce

father's place in the child's life minimizes his loss. His new role must be clearly defined. Time commitments must be honored; even if the father sees the child irregularly, he will maintain the child's trust if he is clear about his availability. It is always better if the child and father work out their relationship together without maternal guidance. The mother's role is to accept and support whatever solution they reach.

Many children idealize their divorced fathers as a way of denying their loss (see below). Such idealization, though often hard for the mother to accept, needs to be respected. Both parents can assist the child in expressing and accepting ambivalent feelings. Tolerance for ambivalence is essential to perceiving the father as a whole person, with both positive and negative qualities.

5. Loss of Environmental Supports.

Many divorcing families move from one home to another. Such a move means the child will lose his familiar surroundings. Most children lose a special room in which was found safety, security, and refuge. Older, more socialized children, lose friends, school, neighboring adults, perhaps youth organizations and leaders. Environmental supports become more meaningful as familiar parental supports disintegrate. Creating new supports, at a time of stress, weakened ability to trust, and negative feelings about oneself, is a difficult task. The effect of these losses can be disabling and should not be underestimated. Divorcing families should not move unless it is essential. If it is essential, staying in the same neighborhood reduces the loss.

6. The Loss of the Pre-Divorce Child.

The child, after family dissolution, is not the same as he was before. So pervasive are the changes in his intimate relationships and environmental supports that his feelings and perceptions of himself and others are profoundly affected.

Children are less secure after divorce. They question, with justification, parental ability to maintain a stable environment. They trust less. Dependency and control relationships become difficult.

One of the major disruptions the child of divorce experiences is a discontinuity in identification. Before the divorce, he had been able to assimilate and integrate qualities from both parents with a reasonable degree of freedom. After divorce, the parents are realistically changed. In addition, the child perceives them differently. Generally one is idealized and the other depreciated. Furthermore, if parents criticize each other, the child may be afraid to identify with qualities formerly deemed acceptable. With these changes in identification models, the child may now reject formerly acceptable parts of himself which are like a parent he now rejects. He may also experience conflicting feelings about qualities that are now unacceptable to one or the other parent because they are reminders of the divorced partner. Conversely, a child may purposely emulate the qualities of one parent to anger the other, or he may seek to become like the absent parent in order to keep the feeling of closeness. Such major identification shifts cause a changed, usually lowered, self-image.

Most children experience an unrealistic sense of guilt and responsibility about the divorce. This contributes to feelings of failure, inadequacy and lowered self-esteem. Before the age of seven, the child's view of justice is one of retribution. He believes anything bad that happens must be punishment for his wrongdoing. Parental quarrels must be about him; the divorce must be his fault. In addition, the child believes that, if his parents loved him, they would reunite; therefore, they don't love him. "Perhaps," he thinks, "I am unlovable. What did I do wrong?" The young child's omnipotent fantasies create a fear of his own power as well as an awareness of helplessness. This issue of power becomes central for the child whose parents divorce during his second through fourth year. At this age, a thought is equivalent to action. To be angry with a parent, to wish him gone, and then to find him in fact gone is translated by the child into, "He left because I got angry." The situation is further complicated for the two- to four-year-old in that he often entertains destructive fantasies when frustrated. His inability to conceptualize future time and permanence leaves him the freedom to say "I'm going to chop you up" with little fear

(Stone and Church, 1968). When, however, loss really occurs, he grows fearful of his anger and magic power. On the other hand, he finds himself powerless to right "his" wrong or to reunite his parents. For example, a thirteen year old girl, whose parents had divorced when she was four, announced to her mother one day, "I guess I won't try to get you and Dad together again." This child had devoted nine years of her life to the accomplishment of an impossible task. She saw herself inadequate and a failure. Indeed, so much of her energy was directed to this hopeless project that she had not developed ego-skills necessary for effective functioning in the real world.

In addition to manipulating to reunite his parents, the child may play one against the other or express anger, when in fact he feels intolerable fear and sadness; as a result, he ends up rejecting parents who care for and love him. He may regress to lower levels of functioning to increase his security. He may feel guilt if his manipulations *are* successful. These manipulations often bring both parental and self-criticism. Thus a negative self-concept is reinforced by those on whom he depends, and with whom he identifies, and by himself. The child who feels himself bad then clings to parents seeking reassurance that he is loved and wanted. Such reassurance, from parents who are so deeply involved in the child's conflicting feelings and manipulations, is seldom meaningful. They often serve only to reinforce his negative self-image.

The stability of the parent-child relationship is threatened by divorce. Before the age of seven, a child thinks in terms of authoritarian morality (Flavell, 1963 and Wolff, 1969). Rules are sacrosanct and cannot be changed. What is right for one person must be right for all. Thus, it is not difficult to conceive that, if it is right to divorce a parent, why is it not right to divorce a child? If one parent can reject the other for "breaking a rule" or being difficult to live with, why could not the child be rejected for exceeding some limit? He also stays out late, gets angry, likes someone besides Mommy or Daddy, and so on. To tell the child he is not divorceable is difficult, for he has effectively been divorced by the parent who has left him. What assurance does he have that his remaining parent will not also leave? In socio-economic settings where foster home or boarding school placement is common, such fears may be quite realistic.

A very complex group of feelings are associated with separation from a person on whom one has come to depend. A child must learn to cope with these feelings as he separates from the symbiotic mother-child relationship, from parents and friends as they come and go, or from toys as they are lost. In an optimal growth situation, short-term separations and minor losses are experienced in such ways that the child learns to deal with the attendant anxiety. Gradually, he learns to depend on his own resources for self-support. He learns to trust that those on whom he depends will be available when needed, even though they are not available all the time. The child from birth through the third year is constantly struggling with the task of separating. Even after this, he remains vulnerable to devastation from major losses until he has developed sufficient ego-strength, self-confidence, interpersonal skills, and support systems outside of the family to feel that he can survive if the parent is not physically available to help him cope with problems. This level of development seldom occurs before the sixth or seventh year. It may never develop for the child who comes from a strife-ridden home, or who has been unable to adjust after overwhelming separations resulting from, for example, major illness, hospitalization, or prolonged parental absence. Also, it may never develop if he perceived the birth of a sibling in terms of parental loss. Separation anxiety assails this weakened child at any age when traumatized by the flood of losses which accompany divorce.

Any separation evolves simultaneously a complex set of emotions. These include, at minimum, love, anger, fear, sadness, helplessness, hopelessness, and—especially for children—guilt.

Love includes feelings of dependency, attachment, and need. Without these feelings no loss would be experienced. Perceived abandonment, hurt, frustration of needs and wants satisfied by the lost person or relationship breed *anger*. *Fear* is experienced in terms of being alone, of further abandonment, of one's own

vulnerability, of the possibility that one's own destructive pow-
ers may have been responsible for the loss. *Sadness*, the hall-
mark of loss, is the feeling when something of value has gone
and can never be again, the sorrow from impoverishment of the
self, the finality of an ending. *Helplessness* is the knowledge
that one is not omnipotent; one did not have the power to prevent the loss. Life will continue without the lost person or relationship. *Hopelessness* is the acceptance of the reality and
finality of the loss. Even if the lost person returns, it is never
the same. The memory and experience of loss alters the relationship. The greatest problem for the post-divorce child is
accepting the hopelessness of reinstating the family. *Guilt*
usually accompanies loss, especially for the child who still believes he is all-powerful. Guilt is proportional to the perception
of his responsibility for the loss and for his wish that the loss
would occur.

How the child copes with this complex set of emotions has
a major effect on his subsequent development. The overwhelming force and confusion of these feelings is often too great and
he turns them off. He detaches emotionally. Sometimes one of
these emotions is more acceptable than the others and this one
dominates when any of the others are felt. Thus, his first response to any emotional stimulus becomes anger or tears or
fear or sometimes even love. A child can seldom deal with this
complex of intense feelings alone. He needs parental support
to allow their full expression, as well as to gain tolerance for
ambivalent feelings.

Parents can provide this support by sharing their own
separation-related feelings with the child. This does not mean
the parent should overwhelm the child with emotion. Rather,
the parent can let the child know he also feels sad, sometimes
scared, and sometimes glad about the divorce; angry and, at the
same time, loving and needing; helpless and struggling; hopeless about the past and hopeful about a realistic future; guilty
and, simultaneously, justified in separating; aware of everyone's pain.

The loss of inner security and sense of self-worth through
divorce is the greatest loss of all. It is also the loss which can

most easily be prevented, given parental awareness and skill in helping the child through this critical experience.

Divorcing parents should be particularly careful of the child two to seven years of age. He needs complete parenting and is unable to understand the complexities of divorce. After seven, the cognitive capacity to understand divorce, strength of identity and sense of autonomy, and supports in the outside world (friends, school), and inner supports (reading, etc.) increase with age. Least affected by divorce is the adolescent, for he is already in the process of separating from his parents.

Divorcing parents will best be able to help the child maintain a positive self-image if they accept his special ways he perceives and conceptualizes events in the outside world, his emotional capacities, and his defense patterns. Such accepting parents will be less reactive to divorce related manipulations, emotional outbursts, and defense maneuvers. The accepting parent can control himself and the child better, help him understand, accept himself, and guide him in ways which will build his self-image.

THE MOURNING PROCESS*

The fact is that a child's parent's divorce is much less important for his future development than how he reacts to the experience. Does he perceive the divorce as a punishment? Does he find the experience overwhelming? Does he compliantly appear accepting while secretly he is angry and too afraid to express anger? Does he rebel openly? Does he manipulate to get his family back together? Does he also expect to be rejected? Does he recognize his losses and mourn them, or does he cover over the pain and leave an empty space inside?

The healthy mourning process involves:

a. Accepting the reality of the loss.

b. Experiencing fully and accepting the complex of feelings which are always associated with loss (love, anger, fear, sadness, helplessness, hopelessness, and sometimes guilt).

---

* For full discussion of the healthy mourning process see Bowlby, 1961; Fenichel, 1945; Jacobsen, 1971; Volkan and Showalter, 1968.

c. Finishing "unfinished business" associated with the loss, i.e., resolving ambivalent feelings, expectations, disappointments, things left unsaid or undone, etc. (Tobin, 1971).

d. Gradually releasing the lost person or relationship. This may be accomplished in active involvement with the separating person if open contact can be maintained. Where loss is sudden and contact is lost, introjecting the lost one or maintaining a fantasy relationship with him gives the mourner time to master the experience. Ties are then gradually cut while strength develops and alternative ways to gratify needs are explored.

e. Establishing new ways to gratify needs.

How Can the Child Be Helped to Complete the Mourning Process?

Acceptance is the essence of healthy mourning. Parents can help the child by accepting their own loss and their own loss-associated feelings. The separation process is essentially the same for all members of the family, even though the specific losses differ. The more deeply the parents explore and understand themselves, the better they will understand and support their child. When both parents address their attention to this process, they form a parent-unit for the child. Such a unit mitigates the loss of the child-mother-father unit of the married family.

The parent will help most by focusing on the reality of the child's feeling about his many losses; these are the most immediate in the awareness of everyone concerned. Feelings may be indirectly expressed, but a parent who is in touch with his own emotional experience will be likely to attend to the underlying "real" feeling. Thus, for example, a child who is fussy after a good day with his father is probably sad and defends against this feeling with anger. It does little good to *ask* a young child what he feels, for he has limited ability to put his deep feelings into words. The empathic parent can look at the child's body, his behavior, and his external situation and make some guess about the child's feelings. In this situation, a conversation might be:

Mother: You looked sad as you came in—before you get angry with me. Did something special happen that made you feel bad?

Child: Oh . . . No . . . We went to the zoo and had chocolate ice cream.

Mother: It must be hard for you to have fun with Dad and then have to leave him. I sometimes feel sad after we have a nice phone conversation. I wish then we could have stayed together. Then I get angry because we couldn't. I almost wish sometimes we didn't have the good times, because I feel lonelier when they are over.

Child: Why can't Daddy come in the house with me when he brings me home?

Mother: Oh. I didn't realize that was important to you.

Child: Well, I asked him to tuck me in bed like he used to, and he said he couldn't come in the house with me.

Mother: I will talk to him about that tomorrow and see what we can do. I can understand that you would like him to tuck you in. It really feels good to have a daddy do that, doesn't it. If you will accept a substitute, I would like to tuck you in tonight while you tell me about the zoo.

By thus focusing on underlying feelings, the child brought to the foreground one of the losses which was important for him, the tuck-in ritual with Daddy. He was able to express his anger about the loss of this child-father interaction. He acted out his ambivalence. It was accepted and a resolution offered. We may assume he felt a sense of rational control over his life and accepted a substitute need—satisfied for the evening. He may also have trusted his parents to work together to give him at least a symbol of something important to him. A fight was avoided and support was given at a crucial time. The child accepted his own needs and feelings as well as effective mothering. Had the mother reacted with anger to his anger, he would have felt less trusting of her sensitivity and caring for him. He would have felt guilty, angry, and afraid at a time when he was especially needy and sad. He probably would have gone to bed pouting, brought his mother back to him with numerous demands (water, blankets, another story, and so on). Perhaps he would have had a nightmare and come to her to relieve his fear.

This issue could have been handled by his father directly. As it was, his mother had to accept the responsibility for dealing with the problem. The father had reinforced his own idealized image as all-giving but failed to deal with the whole child. The following type of father-child interaction would have been appropriate:

Child: Will you come in and tuck me in tonight? You haven't done that for such a long time.

Father: I'd really like that but I don't feel comfortable in the house any more.

Child: But it is still your house. Besides, you told me you were just divorcing mother, that you were not divorcing me. I want you to come in and tuck me in tonight.

Father: Wait a minute. There are about three things going on here. Let's get them straight. First of all, I guess you want me to spend more time with you, or do something that would feel close for both of us. You thought about my tucking you in as a way of doing that. Second, you brought up the whole issue of the divorce and my place in the house and the family now. Third, you became demanding and angry, and I started to get mad about being forced to do something for you.

Child: OK. Forget it.

Father: No, I don't want to forget it. Let's try to work it out. I miss the things we used to do together that just came easily when I was living in the house, like putting you to bed or reading with you or watching TV. I enjoy our Sundays and the zoo was fun, but we don't have much opportunity to just be quiet together. And you and Mommy and I are never together as a family.

Child: The house isn't much fun without you. Mommy is always tired and busy now. And she has that other guy here all the time. If she marries him, you can't ever come back.

Father: Oh, did your wanting me to come in the house have something to do with wanting me to come back to live there?

Child: Well, will you?

Father: No, I won't come back. Mommy and I have found that we are much better off living apart. I know it hurts you and that both Mommy and I lose a lot in our relationship with you. But I also remember how much we used to fight and how afraid you were that we might hurt each other. We weren't very good for you that way, either.

Child: I don't remember the fights very much any more, just the good times. Mommy talks about the fights, but I don't like to listen to her when she does that. She tries to take me away from you. She doesn't want me to like you.

Father: I can't say what Mommy wants or is trying to do. I

think Mommy and I had better get together and work out more of our differences. It sounds as though you are being put in the middle between us, and I don't like to see that. I will call Mommy in the morning.
Child: OK. But what about tonight?
Father: Well, I will go to the door and see if Mommy would object to my putting you to bed tonight. But, I don't think that will solve the whole problem. Next week let's go to my apartment and have a regular "Sunday at home" instead of doing something special.
Child: Could I invite a friend to come along?
Father: Sure. Now I'll go and talk to Mom.

In this interaction, the father was able to set limits on the child. He shared his feelings of loss, he took responsibility for the divorce with his wife, and he relieved the child of the pressure of trying to reunite the family. He took an active role in the family interaction and understood the child's need for closeness with him in a less formal arrangement. The request that a friend join them for the "day at home" is indicative of conflicting feelings about such intimacy. It appears that his son holds unrepressed resentment toward him. He would do well to arrange to wrestle with his child during his day at home or find some other activity that will allow for expression of ambivalent feelings.

By interactions such as the one noted above, communication paths are maintained, trust is built, losses for the child are clarified and defined. The defined loss can be accepted, and substitute gratifications found. Hundreds, perhaps thousands, of such interactions are required to accomplish the task of complete divorce mourning. It must be done over and over again.

It is important to recognize that divorce losses change as the child develops. For example, parents, who remain so estranged that the father is not allowed in the house, will create discomfort for the child at all special events throughout his life where families come together (birthdays, graduations, weddings, etc.). He loses his fantasy of family unity at each of these events.

It is to be hoped that effective parent-child interactions will teach the child to cope with each loss successfully as it comes to awareness. In time he will need parental support only when he is so confused that he cannot sort out the issues himself.

All of us defend against loss because it is overwhelming. Parents must respect the child's perception of his own strength and help him confront reality only when he shows readiness to accept help, much as sexual information is gradually given. He will turn away or misperceive what is said to him if he feels he cannot absorb the reality.

The child needs to finish "unfinished business" with his parents and confront his feelings about them in the present (Perls, 1969; Tobin, 1971). It must be remembered that there are actually great changes in the parents as well as the child as a result of the divorce. Children need to work through their "unfinished business" with the pre-divorce parents in the context of how he was then as well as how he is now. The following example illustrates this point:

> Child: Mom, why don't you ever cook any more?
> Mother: I do cook; I make dinner and breakfast and fix your school lunches.
> Child: But I remember you used to be cooking every day when I got home from school. You made cookies and cakes and things.
> Mother: Oh, that was before the divorce. Now I am at work when you come home from school.
> Child: That is how I always think of you—in the kitchen when I came home from school. I liked the good smells and helping you.
> Mother: Sounds like you really miss that part of me.
> Child: Yes. Like you aren't my mother now, 'cause my mother was always in the kitchen when I got home from school.
> Mother: You sound sad—like you really lost me.
> Child: I am sad—(child hits the sink).
> Mother: Are you angry, too?
> Child: Well—it's not your fault and you had to work.
> Mother: No, it's not my fault, but you can still be angry that I don't have time to bake now and that you feel like you lost your mother.
> Child: I don't feel right getting mad at you. You do so much now. I mean, you work so hard.
> Mother: Are you feeling that I work so hard that you don't get enough mothering now? Like you are deserted now?

Child: Well, it would be nice if we could have more fun. You are always so tired, now.

Mother: I miss the good times we had, too. I remember now that we use to talk a lot when you came home from school. You told me about what you did and I liked baking with you. I have lost touch with that part of you. When I cook dinner now, you are watching TV and I am so rushed to put dinner on the table I don't cook the same things. I remember now that you would chop things for me and stir things that took time. Now I use a lot of frozen food. Asking you to set the table is a lot different from asking you to cook with me. No wonder you resent setting the table now and you didn't before.

Child: I didn't realize the difference either. And I can't talk to you about my stuff anymore. At dinner now you always answer the phone because it might be a date calling. (Child looks away and starts to move away.)

Mother: (Moving toward the child) I feel sad, too. I don't want to lose you in all the changes that have happened since the divorce. Let's sit down now and see how we can get back some of the good things we have had together. Would you sit on my lap for a while?

Child nods ascent and starts to cry.

Too much was brought forth in this interaction to be dealt with at the moment. Sadness, anger, and love were the dominant emotions. The anger was directed both at the mother and at her "dates."

In a therapeutic setting, the child ideally would have hit some mother-symbol (pillow, chair) while the mother held the child so that the complex of feelings, such as love, anger, and hopelessness, could have emerged together. After the feelings had been expressed, the two could more easily find the closeness they once had. Some mothers would be able to cope with such an interaction outside of a therapeutic setting. Mother and child together would mourn the irretrievable loss of the mother-in-the-kitchen-when-I-come-home-from-school ritual, and find another mutually satisfying activity that would allow two-way open communication. The child would also, at some time, deal with feelings of resentment toward the mother's suitors, and the mother's tiredness, and her general unavailability. The child's present needs would be assessed. There may be something particularly difficult to discuss at this time which would have been easier to bring up in the earlier "kitchen" setting. Or, if the time between the remembered interaction and the present is very long, perhaps the child needs some way to regress as a defense against a present stress. The conflict between anger, engendered by frustrated needs for mothering and guilt or over-concern, about her mother's additional burdens, could be explored. No feelings are expressed in the above interaction about either the divorce or the father. Interventions that might have been appropriate include: "If Dad were here, then things would be the same as they used to be." "Sometimes I wish we had never divorced. Things would be easier then." "Even if Dad were still here, I had planned to go to work at this time." Also, no mention was made of possible changes in the child's situation. For example: "Then we were so far from people, you had no one to play with. Now we live in a neighborhood with lots of children and you play after school." "You seemed frightened then and hung on to me a lot. Now you seem to be having more fun with friends. Is that right?"

HOW DOES THE CHILD DEFEND AGAINST LOSS?

Dominant in the constellation of defenses of the child who cannot mourn his losses is either premature detachment or internalization of the lost one or some combination of these.

PREMATURE DETACHMENT (Bowlby, 1961; Deutsch, 1937; Heinicke, 1965) is evidenced by passive withdrawal, active rejection of the lost parent, unusually strong attachment to a substitute, loss of emotionality, or sudden denial of need for the lost relationship. Premature detachment involves a gross distortion of reality—either of the loss itself, or of the child's need for the lost one. Detachment almost always involves a splitting off of intense emotions. It is the most deceptive system, in that parents so easily overlook the child's underlying pain and react to him as if he were not hurt. Communication is thus blocked and the parents, even assuming they are willing and able to help the child, cannot help. What they do say and do is not addressed to the child's pain and thus he finds it irrelevant and frustrating. He concludes, properly, that his parents do not understand him, and so he further detaches himself from what parenting is available. He grows increasingly isolated and lonely.

The only positive aspect of this defense is that the child saves himself from what he perceives as an overwhelming experience. For him, this is a survival maneuver. Indeed, with it he can encapsulate his pain and deal with it at a later time when his ego is stronger and his support system more secure. Thus, we find adults in therapy working through long-buried thoughts and feelings associated with childhood loss (Volkan and Showalter, 1968).

In rejecting the lost parent, the child may also reject those qualities in himself that are like the parent. Such detachment from oneself weakens the child's ego, results in loss of self-esteem and self-awareness, and produces a poor base on which to grow. Some children choose to pattern themselves in any way *but* like the separated parent (develop a negative identification) and thus severely limit growth potential.

Premature detachment from a separated father is likely to result in a too-close relationship to the mother, providing she is available and nurturing. If she is not, the child may detach from her also, continuing to grow virtually parentless.

Parents of children who so defend themselves feel relieved, naively believing that they have easily adjusted. Only some years later do they realize that the child is disturbed and may trace the difficulty back to the time of divorce. The deceptively benign quality of premature detachment is illustrated by the following cases:

> Betty was four when her parents obtained an amicable divorce. She was told her father preferred to live away from home because it was better for his work. She saw him every Sunday. Normally bright and inquisitive, she asked few questions about the change in her family, was easily satisfied by superficial answers, and made no protest about the loss. Apparently she enjoyed the times with her father. He was rather a quiet man who liked to take her to interesting places. She had little difficulty separating from him when he brought her home and she hardly mentioned him between visits. Apparently not concerned about leaving her father, when she left the country with her mother at

the age of eight, she was quite disturbed about leaving her cat. Her relationship with her mother is close and not lacking in emotionality, though anger has not been acceptable in her family. She functions well at school, has few friends. She now suffers from night terrors.

Mrs. I., at forty, has difficulties forming dependency relationships. After her parents divorced when she was seven, she seldom saw her father. Though she remembers their post-divorce relationship clearly, she has almost entirely forgotten their earlier relationship. She is told her pre-divorce relationship with him was very close. He was a "good" father to her. She has few pre-divorce memories of him. She clearly remembers an "embarrassing lack of feeling" when she realized he left home. In later years she came to resent his abandonment, particularly when she was unhappy with her mother. She dislikes those qualities in herself that resemble his. She has difficulty calling him "Daddy," but easily refers to him as "my father." She abhors men who are like her view of her post-divorce father. She is attracted to when who are like her fantasy of her pre-divorce father, thought she cannot form a lasting relationship with them. After the divorce, when her mother had to go to work, she became quite self-sufficient and absorbed in school work. She became outwardly compliant and inwardly rebellious. Her present rigidly independent stance is a defense against her fear of dependency. She trusts nobody, including herself.

The opposite extreme of premature detachment is *internalization* of the person, with the aim of circumventing loss. Internalization may be accomplished by holding a fantasy image of the person or relationship, identifying with him (Krupp, 1954), or introjecting all or parts of him (Perls, 1969). At the extreme he may act as if he is the lost person (Deutsch, 1937). The child who internalizes the lost parent accepts the fact of loss but refuses to allow a new relationship to emerge. He maintains control in a fantasy relationship where, in reality, his control is strictly limited. He continually hopes for something that cannot be. He thus feels frustrated and angry. Underlying his outward appearance of control is his inner awareness of reality and his actual helpless, hopeless position. Internalization of the whole person with both positive and negative qualities is rare. Few children possess tolerance for inconsistency and ambivalence. Therefore, they retain only selected parts that fit a negative or positive image.

Internalization of negative qualities is more likely to occur if the pre-divorce father was feared. The child then gains power and relieves his own fear. A boy, particularly, may internalize his father's sex-role stereotyped behavior in order to resolve conflicts about his own masculinity. If he is not compatible with his mother, he may accentuate his father's negative qualities as a way of punishing her. He may "become" his father to be sent away like his father. Perhaps he takes on his negative qualities in order to force transfer of his custody to the father. Thus he avoids experiencing the guilt involved in actively rejecting his mother.

Internalization of the negative qualities of a parent lead to feelings of insecurity, anxiety, ambivalence, and poor-self image. The child comes to perceive himself as "negative" just as he did the parent internalized. In addition, reactions of others to him are more likely to be negative, and thus his self-image is further devalued and his tendency to be fearful, angry, and defensive is increased.

It appears that most children *internalize an idealized positive image* of a separated father, even though he has been cruel or negligent. I recently asked ten adolescent and adult clients from divorced homes, "How did maintaining an idealized father-image help you?" The replies may be categorized as follows:

1. A denial of the loss: "I could not accept the fact that we would not be together anymore, so I kept him with me all the time. He was like an imaginary companion." "No one so good could have done such a terrible thing as to leave me, so this way I could pretend it was just temporary and he would be back." "I felt I needed a father, I emphasized the parts of him that I wanted in a father and kept him in my mind that way." "I kept them in my mind as together and happy. That way I didn't have to see them apart. I wanted to have a mother-father unit."
2. A source of support: "It really feels good to know that someone always loves you, even if he is 3000 miles away and you only see him once a year." "He was like a Prince Charming who was coming to rescue me." "I kept hope

alive by thinking of him as loving and wanting me." "I felt I always had a haven to turn to, a place to go if things got too bad. Of course, I never tested to find out if he would have had me. Now I can see that he would not have wanted me." "Whenever I had a problem I couldn't solve, I would go to my room and have a fantasy in which he came to me and we talked. I did that until I was sixteen; that is the first time I saw him since I was three. Then, after I saw him, it wasn't so easy because he wasn't like my fantasy, I really felt I had lost something." "I didn't like my mother. This way I had at least one good parent."

3. A boost to self-esteem: "I must be OK if someone so nice cares about me." "No one wants to come from bad parents." "When my mother criticized me, I could keep from hearing her by thinking about my father and that, at least, he really cared so I must not be so bad." "Everybody else had a father. I wanted one too. And mine was better than theirs." "It was like he never left me, so I didn't have to feel guilty about their divorce." "I didn't like myself as a person who thinks bad things about people, especially my father."

4. An identification model: "I was afraid that if I carried around a bad image of him, I would get to be like that. So I kept him 'good.' " "I guess I decided what kind of a father I wanted to have and thought of him that way, and then I identified with that image of him." "I don't understand how I got to be so much like him, since I only saw him a few times a year. Well, I am really more like the way I used to imagine him all the time, not the way I see him now." "I didn't like my mother and I didn't want to be like her, so I purposely imitated the good parts of him." "My mother kept telling me I was just like my father. She meant selfish. I didn't want to believe that, so I kept thinking about the good parts of him to be like."

The child who so idealizes the father may considerably distort reality. For example, one girl whose parents divorced when she was four and a half often talked about the "tradition" she and her father had of eating breakfast together every morning. Actually, the father never woke up before noon and seldom talked to her at all. Her mother's attempts to "help the child to see reality" were met with considerable resistance. Already viewing her mother as a rejecting person (the divorcer) and as denying her what she wanted, she became increasingly convinced of her mother's "badness" and her father's "goodness." She then clung even more tenaciously to the relationship with her still-distant father. With so little support for her idealized image in reality, she lived more and more in fantasy.

The child who idealizes his father often finds himself at cross-purposes with his mother. The mother wants to let the father go; the child wants to keep him. She is uncomfortable with the father's qualities; he accentuates them. The child may become unacceptable to the mother both as a mate symbol and realistically as a difficult child. The child may define as "good" qualities which are questionable. For example, the child may idealize a father's spend-thrift qualities (through which he gets "goodies"), strain the mother's limited resources, clash with her value system, and create distance between mother and child by excessive demand for "things."

The most positive aspect of introjection of the idealized image of the lost parent is that the child takes control of satisfying his own support needs when his parents deny him such support. He refuses to be a helpless victim. Furthermore, he surrounds himself with a warm, loving, caring fantasy. He protects himself until he feels strong enough to accept the more harsh reality.

Problems with this defense arise primarily when the ideal and the real father obviously differ considerably. Contrast, for example, the case of the girl who maintained a fantasy relationship for thirteen years with a father who deserted her when she was three. She had full control of the fantasy relationship and was frustrated only when her mother faced her with "reality." She had the equivalent to a fantasy playmate or a relationship with Santa Claus. At the other extreme, is the case of a girl who saw her father as all-loving and caring and then waited each week for his inconsistent Sunday visit. She often felt betrayed, frustrated, angry, sad, and frightened. She had to repress these feelings in order to maintain her fantasy. The negative feelings were instead turned against her mother, who expressed her resentment at the father's lack of concern.

The child's idealization of the father is the defense most disturbing to the mother. This is particularly true if her own ambivalent feelings are resolved by focusing on her husband's negative qualities (Toomim, 1972).

We may assume that the child himself, while holding onto and becoming like the father, is aware that father was unacceptable. To be like father may threaten his security with his mother. This is particularly true for the child who is told he is "just like his father."

It is difficult for a young child to conceive that parents who are different from each other and who reject each other can both be "good." Therefore, if the father is perceived "good," the mother is likely to be cast in the "not good" position. Parental attempts to manipulate the child's loyalty, to change custody, to get more or give less money, and to communicate with each other through the child, serve to increase his tendency to perceive one good and the other bad. The roles the divorced parents play also support a dichotomized view. The visiting father takes the child places, goes out for dinner with him, makes up for less time by more gifts and generally sees him only when he wants to and is in a relatively good mood. Only the "best" of the visiting father is visible. The mother, on the other hand, increases her role as disciplinarian and has less money to spend than she had when the family was intact. She interacts with the child even when she is tired from working or upset from relationships with other men. She may be seen as rejecting when she pursues her own interests. She is often burdened by her role as single-parent. In addition, she is usually perceived as rejecting or inadequate. The child believes she could have kept Daddy home "if she were better" or "if she wanted to."

Paradoxically, the mother is also a safer person to see as bad, even though rejecting her threatens the child's basic security. The father cannot be taken for granted. He is obviously able to leave and his life is complete in many ways without the child. The child must actively maintain the relationship with him. The child-mother relationship on the other hand is more stable. She has chosen to keep the child, may even have fought for him. Whether she is actually a "good" or a "bad" mother, she is a consistent external support who, by her role, gives him many opportunities to channel his confused feelings and gain a sense of mastery over his pain by struggling with her. He wants his idealized father but she is there. He wants his needs met by him; he accepts need-gratification from her. Father abandons him weekly; Mother stays, and her presence keeps Father away and thus frustrates the child. It is difficult to express anger to a now giving father, easy to be angry with a controlling mother. However he expresses his distress—through anger, withdrawal, projection, etc.—the person who will be most involved in coping with the distress-behavior will be the mother. Her natural reaction to the child's distress may be critical and thus unsupportive. In her own stress, she may not be aware of his deeper needs for security, understanding of his confused feelings, and relief from pain. His distress is generally frustrating to her. Her natural reaction then is likely to further alienate him from her at a time when he needs her most. He is now very likely to react by clinging to her with fear and anger while she reassures him. Still full of hurt and righteous indignation, his ambivalent feelings for her grow and his security is threatened by this interaction.

How Can the Parent Deal With the Child's Defense Behavior?

How the parent deals with the child's defense against the pain of loss is crucial. Confronting the defensive behavior directly tends to make the child *more* defensive. Criticizing his behavior or forcing him to "see reality" will strengthen the defense structure and build his conflictful and negative self-concept. He will turn against his mother and make meaningful communication with her almost impossible. Yet, it is important that the child accept the reality of his situation. Only as he accepts reality will he be able to effectively integrate his experience and his feelings regarding his changing family and self.

The way in which parents help their children cope with the complexities of divorce changes with the child's age. Children too young to express themselves verbally can be approached through play materials. For example, clay can be used to create a variety of family interactions with an unlimited number of characters. Clay also has the advantage of following the young child, who resists directly confronting his divorce trauma, to deal with it indirectly in third person terms.

Doll play, "dress-up," and role-playing are also good ways of helping the young child work through his feelings of loss.* Snapshots of pre-divorce family life may be compiled into a picture story which can be read repeatedly to keep real memories alive and in perspective. Post-divorce pictures from both parent-lines may also be kept to help integrate the changing relationships that occur as he grows, perhaps as parents find other mates. Take pictures of homes, "special" places, toys, friends, ordinary as well as special events, and of course family members. Poses should be natural, not just smiling. This "picture history" gives the child an opportunity to face "reality" as, if, and when he is ready. It reduces his sense of loss.

Finding substitute need-gratification is a highly personal task. The parent can help explore alternatives; only the child can know what alternative will be acceptable. Many parents mistakenly believe a stepparent will replace a natural parent. For many children a stepparent represents a further loss. He may perceive the stepparent as a rival for his natural parents' time and attention; the stepparent may seem to be an intruder into his relationship with his own parents; the new values and new interpersonal structure threatens old accepted and cherished ways. New stepchildren further erode existing family systems. The problem of integrating such an extended family is a major one.

There is a delicate balance between respecting the child's need to defend against painful reality and helping him confront reality when he is ready. Both parents must work together and with the child to help him see reality as he becomes capable of coping with it.

Divorce never eliminates a parent. It only changes the family structure. For better or for worse, a child never loses a

---

* For more details on play therapy and techniqses, see Virginia Axline, *Play Therapy* and also *Dibs, in Search of Self*.

parent totally. He has absorbed, introjected, a part of that parent which will always remain with him whether he keeps a fantasy image of him or a real one.

* * * * * *

I have focused attention on the basic issue of loss from the viewpoint of the child of divorce. No mention has been made of the child who stays with his father or of the influence of siblings. Too little has been said of the effect of mental age and social maturity and of the quality of parent-parent and parent-child relationships as vital factors affecting the child's divorce adjustment. Unfortunately I know of no research which explores these variables. My hope is that the concepts expressed in this paper will stimulate studies which point the way to effective counseling for children of divorce.

REFERENCES

Axline, V.: *Dibs, In Search of Self.* New York, Ballantine, 1964.
Axline, V.: *Play Therapy.* New York, Ballantine, 1969.
Biller, H.: Father absence and the personality development of the male child. *Annual Progress in Child Psychiatry and Child Development.* New York. Brunner-Mazel, 1971.
Bowlby, J.: Process of mourning. *Int J Psychoanal, 42:* 317–340, 1961.
Bowlby, J.: Grief and mourning in infancy and early childhood. *Psychoanal Study Child, 15:* 6052, 1960.
Despert, L.: *Children of Divorce.* New York, Dolp. Doubleday, 1962.
Deutsch, H.: Absence of grief. *Psychoanal Qu, 6:* 12–22, 1937.
Fenichel, O.: *The Psychoanalytic Theory of Neurosis.* New York, Norton, 1945.
Flavell, J.: *The Developmental Psychology of Jean Piaget.* New York, Van N-Rein, 1963.
Heinicke, C.: *Brief Separations.* New York, Int Univ Pr, 1965.
Jacobson, E.: *Depression.* New York, Int Univ Pr, 1971.
Krupp, G.: Identification as a defense against anxiety in coping with loss. *Intl J Psychoanal, 46:* 303–314, 1965.
McDevitt, J. and Settlage, C.: *Separation-Individuation.* New York, Intl Univ Pr, 1971.
Mahler, S.: How the child separates from mother. *The Mental Health of the Child.* Rockville, Md., National Institute of Mental Health, 1971.
Perls, F.: *Ego, Hunger and Aggression.* New York, Random, 1968.
Perls, F.: *Gestalt Therapy Verbatim.* Ogden, Utah, Real People, 1969.

Siggin, L.: Mourning: A critical review of the literature. *Intl J Psychoanal, 17:* 14025, 1963.

Stone, J. L., and Church, J.: *Childhood and Adolescence.* New York, Random, 1968.

Tobin, S.: Saying goodbye in gestalt therapy. *Psychotherapy, 8:* 150–155, 1971.

Toomim, M.: Structured separation with counseling: a therapeutic approach for couples in conflict. *Family Process, 11:* 299–310, 1972.

Volkan, V.: Normal and pathological grief reactions—a guide for the family physician. *Va Med Mon, 93:* 651–656, 1966.

Volkan, V.: Typical findings in pathological grief. *Psychiatr Qu, 44:* 231–250, 1970.

Volkan, V. and Showalter, C.: Know object loss, disturbance in reality testing and "re-grief" work as a method of brief psychotherapy. *Psychiatr Qu, 42:* 358–374, 1968.

Wolff, S.: *Children Under Stress.* London, Penguin, 1969.

CHAPTER 6

PROBLEMS OF FAMILIES IN CRISES

GILBERT L. INGRAM *

● ●

HISTORICAL PERSPECTIVE ON THE FAMILY

THE FAMILY AND DELINQUENCY

WORKING WITH THE FAMILY IN CRISIS

THE FUTURE

REFERENCES

● ●

THE FAMILY as a viable social unit is under attack from many different sources in modern American society. The assaults have increased in both intensity and number, ranging from criticism concerning the family's lack of effectiveness in producing adaptable members of society, to demands for elimination of the family as it is presently constituted (Cooper, 1970). An immediate result of these assaults is exemplified in the present chapter; many researchers and practitioners are being compelled to look closely at what is happening.

The spectacle is depressing and indeed presents a sad commentary on the family's efficacy as a social unit. Because 50

---

* This chapter represents opinions of the writer and does not represent official policy or attitudes of the Federal Bureau of Prisons or the United States Public Health Service.

percent of delinquents come from broken homes, the fact that families are increasingly being broken by desertion and divorce is of immediate concern. Of those units that manage to remain intact, the adult family members manifest their social and emotional problems in various ways, such as alcoholism, drug addiction, crime, and suicide. These problems naturally extend to children of the unhappy families.

Past dissatisfactions of observors toward the family generally were aimed at the lower class of society and thus were more easily dismissed as problems peculiar to that segment of the population. Today, the delinquent products of inadequate, unstable family units are visible in every social class and cannot be so easily ignored.

Theorists and practitioners of diverse persuasions seem to agree that the family is of fundamental importance in the occurrence of delinquency. Every involved discipline, despite differences in emphasis, joins in the general castigation of the family. Typical of these views are the following: It is a truism that for every juvenile delinquent, there is a delinquent home environment. Children are not born delinquent; they are made that way by their families, usually by their parents (CRM's *Developmental Psychology Today* 1971, p. 291). The more thorough a study of juvenile delinquency is, the greater the emphasis laid on the family as a social unit (Pettit, 1970, p. 191).

The family is frequently cited as the villain of many social evils but with regard to delinquency there is almost unanimous agreement. Even in those cases in which other economic, cultural and psychological factors play a major role, the family still remains significant by its failure to counteract these other forces.

Research results notwithstanding, it is possible that this consensus is nothing more than an empty generalization, devoid of any real meaning and worthless for purposes of prevention or treatment. In fact, such a broad indictment of the family may seduce some into thinking that they now understand the problem when, obviously, this is not the case.

Another fallacy in this area is the tendency to use preliminary research results to place a label on a family that seems to breed delinquency. Once this label is available, the assumption is made that a grasp on the cause of delinquency is at hand. Hypostatization is a comforting but nonproductive enterprise. The causes of delinquency are undoubtedly complex and varied and not unitary.

It is not the intention to present a comprehensive review of all literature pertaining to the effect of the family on delinquent behavior. This task, although necessary, has been accomplished by others, including an excellent review by Peterson and Becker (1965). Rather, the goal is an overview of the area emphasizing general conclusions that appear to have some merit and, more importantly, that may have some applicability. Problems in working with the families of delinquents are discussed and specific examples of tactics are presented that may facilitate successful intervention.

HISTORICAL PERSPECTIVE ON THE FAMILY

The modern concept of childhood was unknown in the Middle Ages. At that time, childhood was viewed exclusively as a transition stage before adulthood. As the rate of infant mortality and the demand for productive work decreased, the family began to focus on the child as an individual in his own right. Children were able to go to school and refrain from work. Especially during the Seventeenth and Eighteenth Centuries with the increased opportunity for education, childhood assumed the status of a separate stage of development. Adolescence as a separate stage was even later in evolving, not appearing in its present state until the late Nineteenth and early Twentieth Centuries.

During most of the Nineteenth Century, the agrarian-based culture predominated with its independent family unity and a cohesive community life. As the industrial culture grew, family structure loosened with the concentration of populations in the large, heterogeneous communities. The shift was not only rural to urban, but also included an increased immigration from Europe to the big cities of this country. It should be noted that separate courts for juveniles were first established in the late

Nineteenth Century after the large metropolitan courts were swamped with an increasing number of juvenile offenders.

Long cited as a puzzling and difficult stage, adolescence gained society's concentrated attention after the late Nineteenth Century. Because of the rapid technological advances and the influence of mass media, the present situation provides even more stress for the teenager and the family. As Mead aptly stated, "Parents have been rearing unknown children for an unknown world since about 1946 (Mead, 1972, p. 586)."

Added to the ordinary pains and adaptations that occur in growing up during any historical period, today's teenager is placed in various conflict situations. While being bombarded with provocative stimuli and the sight of hedonistic behaviors of adults, the adolescent is taught to remain economically unproductive and to postpone immediate satisfaction for long range goals. Yet, after a prolonged period of protection and abstinence from "adult" activities, he is supposed to emerge somehow from this dependent status into adulthood fully capable of behaving in a responsible manner. Added to these contradictory messages, which confuse and frustrate most adolescents, are the other social changes that have altered family life.

The size of the typical family has decreased so that each member is interacting with fewer other members, making individual contributions all the more important. At the same time, shared family activity or "togetherness" has diminished, and this restricts the number of intrafamilial interactions. This trend sometimes prevents the family's carrying out its prescribed social function. The once biological contribution of the family was that of providing economic and physical safety for the members. Today, society expects the family to serve primarily as a socialization mechanism for the child and to provide satisfaction of psychological needs for all family members.

Leadership of the family has shifted in many ways from a patriarchal type to a more democratic or shared method of decision making. The former role of the father, that of providing explicit authority and fulfilling visible economic duties, allowed the children to model after him. He was quickly accepted as the authority figure. The mother's role was also definite and visible. Changing roles plus the extensive impact of mass media have created a situation in which children are less likely to accept the parents as models of behavior. Riesman (1969) has written of the increasing separatism of teenage culture and the massing in schools of large numbers of young people. The atmosphere engendered by this phenomenon is one of questioning the legitimacy of adult authority. In fact, Riesman believes that the young become "captives" of each other.

The shift in parental roles also has direct effects on the child when problems occur between the parents. One immediate result is seen in the handling of child custody cases. Until recently, fathers were considered to own all family property, including the children. The mother for all practical purposes had no legal rights to them. Today, an almost automatic preference obtains for the mother over the father in such court decisions.

Another characteristic of modern families is their increased mobility. Many writers describe families as completely inefficient social units, citing the nomadic nature of their existence and resultant lack of stability. All of these modern trends in the life style of family units have dramatic effects on the children. The small size of the family plus the frequent changes in residence creates a lack of personal ties with others. Most modern families work and recreate as separate individuals outside of their home neighborhood. It is no great surprise that children of such families feel alienated, disenchanted, and at odds with the world around them.

Granted that modern families have unique problems and do not seem to be satisfying society's expectations. Why, though, do seemingly privileged teenagers become delinquent, especially in terms of violent acting-out behavior? The attribution of such behavior to lower-class versus middle-class persons had been accepted as a general belief in both lay and professional circles. More recently, Stark and McEvoy (1972) among others have challenged this assumption. Using data compiled by the National Commission on the Causes and Prevention of Violence, they cited statistics supporting the idea that, in fact, the middle class is more prone toward physical assault than the poor. Stark and McEvoy suggested that violence among the poor is more likely to become a police matter because of lack of privacy and little recourse to professional counselors or influential friends.

Keniston (1968) has cited one reason for some of the problems of modern families that offers a different perspective on violence. The adolescent's constant exposure to social upheavals occurring during the past decades has afforded an excellent opportunity for disagreeing with parental values and for perceiving between what parents say and what they do. Keniston acknowledged that there has always been a failure to live up to professed ideals, but heretofore the adolescent has learned when parents can be reasonably expected to practice what they preach. Today, this "institutionalization of hypocrisy" does not occur so easily because rapid social change does not allow for the easy definition of exceptions to the rule and it is much easier for youth to detect such discrepancies. Ironically, the young hold to those values (love of fellow man, equality for all) which their parents espouse but do not practice. Having been raised in an affluent environment, the adolescent feels outrage over the lack of opportunities for those less fortunate. Added to this general feeling of anger and disappointment with his parents is the ever-present fear caused by the threat of the bomb and possible technological death. The awareness of violence is continually reinforced by frequently publicized mob behaviors.

Whether the cause is frustration over living conditions, personal inadequacies, or, as Keniston has suggested, an obsession concerning violence in general, there is little doubt that the tendency to act out antisocially is increasing among youth in all social classes.

Today, if the family were considered to be a small business enterprise, it might have to declare bankruptcy. The task of turning out a useful social product is not being accomplished. In a recent large-scale study, the authors concluded that most teenagers do not achieve emotional autonomy, detachment from the family, or a personal ethical code of behavior (Douvan and Adelson, 1966). Although these manifestations of inadequate families are possibly as significant as delinquency, none produce such immediate and tangible damage against society. While the financial cost of delinquency is astronomical by all estimates, the psychological and sociological effects are undoubtedly a greater liability for everyone.

THE FAMILY AND DELINQUENCY

Numerous studies have been conducted in the investigation of family characteristics and delinquent behavior. Too many of these studies suffer from severe methodological weaknesses. The typical strategy used in those studies that seem to satisfy research requirements has been a comparison of families of delinquents with families of nondelinquents. The shotgun approach has been necessary because no systematic theory is available to guide inquiry and to organize existing data. The growing emphasis on differential classification programs and the concomitant development of differential treatment approaches acknowledge what every practitioner knows; i.e. delinquents do not present themselves as a homogeneous group for research or treatment purposes. Similarly, families of delinquents have their own particular "personality" and do not as a single group share similar characteristics.

Rubenfeld (1967) identified the lack of a framework for family classification as a serious drawback in any attempt to determine the effect of family life on delinquent behavior. However, his suggestion for categorizing families by use of child-rearing patterns, such as those determined by the Fels Institute, may also be a waste of time. For example, after reviewing the enormous amount of data on the effect of different child-rearing practices, McCandless (1967) presented his advice which seems most appropriate:

> . . . . . mothers [parents] who are well-meaning and who try relaxedly to do what they sincerely believe is best for their children—particularly when this is in harmony with the cultural ways of the community with which they are most closely associated—obtain the best results with their children (McCandless, 1967, pp. 127–128).

We have little reliable data on the subject considering the widely scattered attention directed toward it.

Despite the lack of information concerning the family, research findings have indicated possible characteristics that may bear on the problem. Three general types of families have consistently been identified with delinquent behavior: an unhappy, disrupted home with poor structure; a home in which parental attitudes of rejection prevail; and homes demonstrating a lack of consistent and adequate discipline. Whenever possible, representative studies from both the earlier and the more current literature are presented.

Disrupted Homes and Delinquency

Families may be disrupted by the physical loss of a member through death, divorce, or separation, or by the lack of structure caused by disturbed or criminalistic parents. Many studies in this area have been devoted to the effect of father absence on delinquent males, but the investigation of that variable has been a recent phenomenon.

A widely held assumption had been that the mother produced the major effect on the children and the father was relatively unimportant. Freud's writings were largely responsible for this focus on the mother's role, and even his critics seemed to agree with him on this one issue. The effect of maternal deprivation dominated the literature for many years. However, as more interest developed concerning the father's role, studies began to demonstrate the influence of the father, particularly concerning delinquency. Glueck and Glueck (1962) cited repeated instances of alcoholism, nonsupport, brutality, and frequent absence from home in the fathers of delinquent fathers. Extreme difficulties with male authority figures were frequently noted (*see* Medinnus, 1965) but disturbed relations with mothers were present only for a few delinquents (Brigham, Rickets, & Johnson, 1967).

As attention was directed more toward the father, new problems were encountered which interfered with research. If the family is intact, fathers usually work during the day and have to be contacted on evenings or weekends. Because this involvement entails the loss of leisure time, fathers are less likely to cooperate. Fathers also view themselves as having little to do with their children's problems because they share the same cultural bias that others have. If the father is unavailable, researchers have frequently adopted another approach which has severe limitations; namely, interviews are held with the mother to obtain information about the father. Distorted perceptions are typically obtained, either positively biased when the home is intact or negatively biased when the home is broken. Both kinds of distortions interfere with comparisons of fatherless homes and intact homes.

Available data from those studies that have been conducted on the effect of fatherless homes indicate that the way in which the father leaves the family is an important variable. For example, loss of either parent through death does not seem to be as harmful an experience as a separation because of parental discord.

When the father is absent from the home, the effect apparently centers on disturbed social behaviors for boys. Father absence produced poor sex typing (Bach, 1946) and poor social relations (Stolz, 1954). Because these factors have been associated with delinquency, the effect of father absence on delinquent behavior seems quite important. The question of the relation of the child's age when father absence occurs to subsequent delinquent behavior is another issue far from being settled. Lynn and Sawrey (1959) and Siegman (1966) found that father absence before age five often produced compensatory masculine behavior in adolescence. More recently, Biller (1971) reviewed the literature and concluded that absence during the elementary school years was most important for the development of delinquency.

The importance of father absence for delinquency is not limited to lower class children. Siegman (1966) asked a group of medical students anonymously to reveal their early histories. Minor behavior problems such as cheating in school were equally likely to occur in both father-absent and father-present groups, but serious acts such as theft of property occurred more frequently in the father-absent group.

Recognizing the importance of a variable and isolating its particular effect are two entirely different problems. Although many studies do support the notion that fatherless homes frequently result in delinquency, approaching the problem simply in terms of father-absence versus intact homes has yielded no definitive answers. Hertzog and Studia (1968) reviewed fifty-nine studies dealing with the effects of fatherlessness on children in general and thirteen studies dealing directly with delinquency. They found general support for a relationship between delinquency and fatherless homes but also noted qualifying factors. Their suggestions for future research included a shift from single variable analysis to a study of interacting clusters of factors. The fact that approximately six million children in the United States are being raised in fatherless homes indicates the urgency of proceeding with definitive studies.

Contrary to earlier writings, absence of the mother is not frequently cited as a major factor in the area of delinquency. Most researchers apparently agree with Becker, Peterson, Hellmer, Shoemaker, and Quay (1959) who reported the role of the father as being apparently more important than that of the mother in the development of delinquent behavior. More recently, as the role of the mother has shifted in our society, some attention has been directed toward the possible influence of working mothers on children. However, most studies indicate that that type of temporary absence is not a significant factor.

Emotional disturbance on the part of either parent, which also produces a lack of structure in the home, seems to be instrumental in producing disturbed delinquents. Delinquents who are regarded as emotionally disturbed often have disturbed parents (Becker, *et al.*, 1959; Liverant, 1959; Peterson, Becker, Hellmer, Shoemaker, and Quay, 1959; Richardson & Roebuck, 1965). Many practitioners have discovered that delinquents have character-disordered parents when they attempted unsuccessfully to work with them (Reiner and Kaufman, 1959). The presence of disturbed or criminalistic parents does not distinguish delinquents from other groups, but it does indicate that homes disrupted by disturbed as well as absent parental figures may indeed contribute to antisocial behavior.

Homes also may be disrupted by the lack of physical space

and by the chaotic life style that accompanies such an environment. These characteristics typically describe the lower class family, but as already stated, lack of structure is not confined to the physical aspects of the home. In this sense, middle-class children also are often exposed to a living style that precludes a stable pattern of existence. One immediate result of such disrupted homelife for children from all social classes is to make them more vulnerable to the influence of antisocial peer group (Peterson and Becker, 1965).

The specific ways in which broken and disrupted homes contribute substantially to the delinquency problem are just beginning to be identified. For example, Wood, Wilson, Jessor, and Bogan (1966) found that the overwhelming feelings of powerlessness that delinquents have in dealing with society can be attributed partly to the lack of meaningful structure in their family life. As yet, few research findings in this area have been substantiated and none have been shown to offer meaningful ideas for application in the real world.

Parental Rejection and Delinquency

Rejection of the child by either or both parents has long been cited as one important factor in aggressive behavior by numerous researchers. For instance, Updegraff (1939), in reviewing the literature concerning the influence of parental attitudes upon the child's behavior, found a positive relation between maternal rejection and overt aggression in the child. Similarly, Baldwin, Kalhorn, and Breese (1945), using data from Fels project, found that rejected children showed a marked tendency toward quarreling, increased resistance toward adults, and sibling hostility. Bandura and Walters (1959) and Andry (1960) found rejection by the father to be a significant pattern for their delinquent samples. McCord, McCord, and Howard (1961) conducted an extensive study involving direct observations of behavior for more than five years. One of their relevant findings was that parents who generally rejected their sons were most likely to produce aggressive boys. More recently, McCord, McCord, and Howard (1963) suggested that antisocial aggression depends more on the degree of rejection and other parental behaviors than simply the absence or presence of parental rejection.

A great deal more has been written about the effect of parental rejection on a particular type of delinquent or criminal, namely the psychopath. This cruel, defiant person who personifies the layman's stereotype for all delinquents deserves some special attention because he exhibits extreme variations of behavior found in many delinquents.

Lipman (1951) presented a view which may be taken as a general orientation. He said that the psychopathic child is one who has been rejected from the beginning. Subsequent aggression is almost a compulsive act and no feeling for other people is present. Bender (1961) stated that psychopathic behavior occurs when the child is exposed to early and severe emotional and social deprivation attributable either to impersonal institutional care or to critical blocks in the mother-child relationship. Fox (1961) proposed that the psychopath's lack of internalization of cultural values could result from his unfortunate first contact with society, i.e. extreme rejection by the parents.

This has an interesting analogy in research conducted on animals. Harlow (1962) found that monkeys raised in isolation had severe social abnormalities that could be compared to psychopathic behavior. Among other types of behavior, they showed exaggerated aggression and an absence of affectional interaction. This seems to indicate that the influence of early social relationships on aggressive behavior may hold despite species differences.

Psychopathic behavior has been proposed to stem from parent-child relationships other than extreme rejection. Greenacre (1945) reported the fathers of psychopaths to be usually men who spend little time at home and who act in a cold manner toward the child. The mother was not a steady parent in her interactions with the child or with others. Jenkins (1960) proposed in addition to the possibility of organic involvement, that the child may have been exposed to a confusing situation for social training. All of these proposals are generally in agreement with the research cited above. Despite the post facto nature of the writings, they point to a rejecting environment early in life as a causal factor in aggressive behavior and possibly in the etiology of psychopathy.

Parental Control Techniques and Delinquency

There are three general ways in which parental reactions seem to contribute to delinquency: (1) Parental attempts at discipline are inadequate to control antisocial behavior; (2) Parental reactions provide a punitive model for the child to imitate; and (3) The parents deliberately encourage the child's inappropriate behavior.

The inadequacy of parental discipline in controlling the delinquent's behavior has been noted by many researchers. Healy and Bronner (1926) and Burt (1929) noted that defective parental discipline was an important social determinant of delinquent behavior. Merrill (1947) determined that most of her delinquents came from homes with lax, erratic, or overly strict discipline, Glueck and Glueck (1950) found that the delinquent's parents, particularly the father, had the same difficulty with discipline. Bandura and Waters, (1959), Bennett (1960), and McCord, *et al.*, (1961) cited the inconsistent handling of problem behavior by parents as a factor in delinquency.

The effect of inadequate discipline is hypothesized by Hoffman and Saltzstein (1967) to be the weak development of conscience frequently found in delinquents. Apparently the type of discipline exerted by the parents does not facilitate the increased resistance to temptation which is necessary to prevent antisocial acts.

The second way in which parental control techniques may lead to delinquency is by providing an aggressive model for the child. Bandura, Ross, and Ross (1961, 1963) found that children, especially boys, are influenced by viewing aggressive behavior, and more importantly, become more aggressive themselves in other situations. The significance of these studies is magnified by the fact that parents of delinquents resort more often to aggressive behavior for punishment than do other parents (Glueck and Glueck, 1950, McCord, *et al.*, 1961).

Physical punishment may effectively suppress behavior for a short period but it frequently causes a great deal of frustration and provides another opportunity for the delinquent to learn to be aggressive. As Sears, Maccoby, and Levin (1957) found in their classic study, the pattern of child-rearing that produces the most aggressive children is when the parents disapprove of aggression but punish its occurrence with their own physical aggression or threats of aggression.

The third, and perhaps most insidious manner by which parents may influence the expression of delinquency, is the deliberate encouragement of antisocial acts. A great deal of data has been collected which supports the hypothesis that delinquent behavior is reinforced by the family. Shaw and McKay (1942) and Glueck and Glueck (1950) both found that their delinquents came from homes in which other criminals were living. McCord and McCord (1958) discovered that a criminal father plus the absence of maternal warmth was the one combination most likely to lead to delinquent behavior. Similarly, dropping out of school, which typically accompanies delinquency, is related to the parents exhibiting the same behavior (Williams, 1963).

The above examples of general reinforcement of delinquency are overshadowed by the occurrences of direct antisocial instruction by the parents. Bandura and Walters (1959) noted that parents of aggressive boys tended to encourage aggression. Bandura (1960) found that mothers of aggressive boys were punitive when aggression was expressed toward them but became more tolerant when the aggression was expressed toward peers or siblings. Becker, Peterson, Luria, Shoemaker, and Hellmer (1962) reported that mothers who frequently used physical punishment also frequently told their children to fight other children whenever necessary.

WORKING WITH THE FAMILY IN CRISIS

Although increasing evidence indicates that families are doing a poor job of rearing children, one conclusion remains inevitable under our present system of justice; the family can not be ignored in either the prevention or treatment of delinquents.

In reviewing the history of the development of juvenile courts in this country, Mennel (1972) concluded:

Today, as then, we can no longer disqualify parents from caring for their children simply because they are poor or unfamiliar with the principles of child psychology. Parents may indeed abuse or fail to exercise their disciplinary authority. There is, however, little historical evidence to indicate that public authorities in the United States have provided viable and humane alternatives [Mennel, 1972, p. 78].

Until realistic alternatives are available or society changes its viewpoints regarding the sacrosanctity of the family, involvement of the family is necessary. Even after the delinquent's behavior has become completely unmanageable, the situation in which he does not have to return to his basic family unit would be the rare exception. Unfortunately, even in this case or after incarceration has been effected, the courts have no legal authority to insist upon the parent's involvement in the treatment of the child.

Experience to date indicates that successfully involving the family in the prevention or treatment of delinquency often is dependent upon the individual expertise and initiative of the change agent in overcoming bureaucratic inertia. Few specific suggestions are available from the research literature. However, a full understanding of many of the problems facing the family in crisis better prepares the worker to facilitate this involvement. Several parental reactions to delinquency occur frequently enough to warrant some attention. These reactions include a denial of blame with subsequent anger directed toward society, guilt after-the-fact and a feeling of helplessness, and finally, passivity and a relinquishing of responsibility because it is now out of their hands.

The Hostile Family

Many families confronted with the fact of their child's delinquency react very negatively. Typically, these are multiproblem families for whom delinquency poses an additional crisis. Already overwhelmed with financial and social misfortunes, the family is ill-prepared to deal realistically with the child's situation. Most hostile families fall into society's lower social classes.

Previous interactions between family members and society's representatives usually have been in relation to problems in the educational system and frequently have been negative experiences. Against this background, the appearance of another "helper" in the life of the family may be greeted with anger and sometimes overt hostility. Communication often breaks down because of real differences which exist between the values and language of the worker and the family.

Not only do the disadvantaged have their own particular vocabulary and style of speech, but their concerns in life may differ significantly from the middle-class culture (Miller, 1958). Typical middle-class workers, regardless of discipline, probably share common beliefs about human nature (Dole & Nottingham, 1969). Frequently, the workers' beliefs conflict with the family's own values and communication channels break down. For example, the middle-class emphases on frugality and responsibility probably are not shared by disadvantaged families. Similarly, the family may seem unconcerned with long-term plans because their energies are focused on present problems. Confronted with an unwelcome stranger who talks differently and places a high value on the "wrong" things, family members may directly indicate their disagreement and displeasure. Any helper, finding his well-intentioned overtures greeted thus, can fall into the trap of assuming an authoritative posture and a condescending manner. The interaction undoubtedly will proceed downhill from this point.

What can be done to work with such a family? The answer depends upon the ability of the helper to understand and accept the members for what they are. This means that he must entertain the idea that the family's behaviors and values may be appropriate *for them*. If he can do that, he should aim at the facilitation of the child's adaptation by working with the family. This process entails his gaining acceptance not as a friend but as someone who can help. Learning the language and values of the family are important because it is the rare middle-class person who fully appreciates the social and personal lives of the lower-class individual. Other suggestions that may be of some use include the following:

(1) Any indications of talking down to the family will reinforce their dislike and distrust of the authority person.

(2) Refusing to state opinions or backing down when confronted by the family will be interpreted as a sign of weakness and interfere with rapport.

(3) Avoidance of some relevant issues for the sake of "being nice" will destroy any respect for the person.

(4) Firmness, not coldness, is the preferred approach.

(5) Programs and suggestions should be geared to the real concerns of the family and not for abstract goals.

(6) Giving the family concrete tools to work with is better than speaking in generalities.

(7) Providing the family with tangible services, if at all possible, will facilitate their cooperation.

(8) Do not expect appreciation, at least in the traditional sense, for these efforts.

Most of these suggestions are self-explanatory. Providing concrete suggestions (Number 6 above) is discussed in the next session. An example of a tangible service (Number 7 above) may be the worker's serving as a go-between for the family and the school.

After the disadvantaged child has experienced difficulties in school, attempts by either the teacher or the parent to intervene are usually viewed as interference by the other party. An increasingly negative series of communications may convince the family, for example, that the teacher is either not concerned or is discriminating unfairly against the child. Subsequent school difficulties may be excused by the parents in such an atmosphere of distrust. Serving as a go-between in this case, the worker can make a valuable contribution by soliciting information from the school and by sharing helpful family data with the teacher. One result of such activities may be to discover that the child, accidently or deliberately, has reinforced erroneous assumptions on the part of both teacher and parents. Regardless of the specifics, however, all parties benefit from this type of interchange which minimizes the defensive maneuverings of all concerned.

The best intentions will not always guarantee success in working with the family, especially one predisposed to suspicion and hostility toward outsiders. The practitioner may well find that his contributions are either not accepted or are of limited usefulness. This outcome should suggest another immediate alternative which has proven effective in many instances, namely the use of the community volunteer.

Initial reluctance to use volunteers was a natural reaction from professionals who felt that they and only they could understand and deal with delinquents and their families. However, with the failure of traditional therapy approaches and the scarcity of professionals, the use of lay counselors or family workers has gained in popularity. Using volunteers does not remove the responsibility from the worker. Rather, the professional becomes a case manager at a different level; for example, selection, assignment, and training of volunteers is essential for the success of a volunteer program. If done correctly, the use of volunteers can be effective even in the most difficult situations. Carkhuff (1971) has described a successful program to train lay counselors indigenous to the inner-city, typically regarded as one of the most resistive areas to reach with any services.

The Inadequate Family

One frequently finds families that want to cooperate but seem incapable of handling their children or at least have difficulty with one particular child. Sometimes the family has reared several children without delinquent histories but another child has run into numerous difficulties. This child may be a special child in that he has been sickly, retarded, brain damaged, left alone for a period because of unavoidable environmental circumstances, or, for one reason or another, has been afforded special status in the parent's eyes. The inappropriate handling of such a child may lead to delinquency in any social class. Patterson, Cobb, and Ray (1970) found that the types of processes in the family leading to delinquent behavior were present in all socioeconomic levels.

Assuming that the family does want to help their child or that the worker has prepared them for such involvement, the task of the practitioner is to deliver as quickly as possible to the parents techniques for making successful changes in the child's behavior. For reasons both of efficacy and efficiency, behavioral techniques seem to be the treatment of choice. They are the easiest to communicate, easiest to understand, and have been applied successfully with parents in diverse situations. Using the family itself as an agent of social change allows them to assume primary responsibility for the child which enhances feelings of competence and mastery over their environment. Additionally, the techniques are already being used by the parents but typically in an unsystematic fashion. Minuchin, Montalvo, Guerney, Rosman, and Schumer (1967) discovered that the mothers of problem children in slum areas used reinforcement techniques, but inconsistently and inappropriately for the child's deviant behavior.

Some direct results of inappropriate reinforcement techniques on delinquents have been identified. Delinquents, in comparison to nondelinquents, are raised in homes where dependency behavior, approval seeking, and verbalizations of dependent behavior are negatively reinforced (Bandura and Walters, 1969; Bender, 1947; McCord and McCord, 1956). The implications of this extinction of dependency behavior for verbal counseling approaches may explain in part the fact that delinquents do not typically profit from conventional therapy. In fact, Mueller (1969) found that client's behaviors with therapists became increasingly similar to behaviors that occurred within the family constellation.

The strategy of retraining parents to act as more effective behavior modifiers has been successfully applied to parents of disturbed children (Hirsch and Walder, 1969). The basic idea of using parents as the primary change agents is not only more economical and practical, but Patterson, *et al.* (1970) cited evidence suggesting that it may have a more permanent effect. Their program, in contrast with other attempts, concentrated on changing multiple classes of deviant child behaviors rather than altering a single behavior. Some of their specific techniques and findings have wider applicability for working with parents than their particular study. Relevant suggestions from their program are summarized below.

(1) Having parents simply read programmed texts on child management techniques is of limited value. [As adjunct material, these books may be helpful: *Child Management*, Smith and Smith, 1966; *Living with Children*, Patterson and Gullion, 1968.]

(2) Telling parents what to do is not as effective as the actual demonstration of recommended procedures.

(3) Training of the parent in the home has the advantage of the normal setting but it is a costly procedure. Group training methods are more advantageous once the family becomes involved in the process.

(4) Parents are notoriously inaccurate in remembering their children's early behaviors. Dependable information should be obtained through ongoing recording.

(5) Structuring of home visits is necessary to get an adequate observation of the home. Family members often attempt to avoid the 'intruder' by remaining in an inaccessible location such as the bedroom. It may be necessary to specify requirements of who is to be present and where during these visits.

(6) Observing the behavior of the delinquent by himself is less reliable than watching the behavior of all family members for a period of time.

(7) The verbal behavior of parents (everything is fine now; yes, we understand the problem, etc.) should not be accepted at face value without additional evidence of changes in behavior.

(8) Providing concrete examples of how to apply behavior principles to everyday problems is more easily understood by parents than the supplying of textbook answers.

(9) It may be necessary to become a nuisance to the father in order to obtain his cooperation, i.e. contact him

daily, have court personnel call him, etc. The worker should keep in mind that the uncooperative father may be unable to carry out his assigned tasks rather than being deliberately resistive.

(10) The parent's starting with a simple behavioral problem between himself and the child maximizes the probability of a successful experience with the techniques.

(11) One goal of family training is to teach the parents to intercede before the child's behavior becomes extreme and before physical measures are necessary to control it.

(12) Parents should be reassured that an improvement in the behavior of one child does not mean that another child will increase his deviant behavior. Many parents believe this to be true and sometimes are reluctant to initiate change.

The Family of the Incarcerated Delinquent

After delinquency has progressed to the point requiring institutionalization, it is exceedingly difficult to involve the family in rehabilitation of the delinquent. In addition to the predisposing circumstances which may have existed in the family for some time, the incarceration of the child creates additional problems for the family. Many families react very negatively to the institutionalization, preferring to act as if the problem no longer belongs to them. Others use the physical separation as an excuse to justify feelings of rejection that may have originally contributed to the delinquency. Regardless of the underlying factors, it is imperative that staff members attempt to overcome this obstacle to rehabilitation.

Staff time is not sufficient to allow for home visitation, not to mention the expense involved in such activities. Encouraging the family to meet with staff on institutional visiting days has not proven successful. Unless the family is able to afford weekday trips, which would be most unusual, visits mean weekend hours and the resultant absence of key staff members. Moreover, even when all parties are present, family involvement through visits is not regular enough for meaningful interactions to occur. All of these factors add to the communication gaps and lead to misconceptions for both staff and family. The delinquent suffers directly from the lack of family involvement because parental planning is crucial for release programming but, more importantly, because the parent's behavior often has been a contributing factor to the delinquent's present situation.

One recent suggestion has been to invite groups of parents of delinquents to the institution for week-long visits (Stollery, 1970). Teams of staff counselors evaluate the delinquent's behavior and plan a unified program for him in conjunction with all family members. This program has the added advantage for low income families of providing a type of family vacation as contrasted with the brief, intermittent visits which may serve as a financial punishment. When groups of parents visit at the same time, it serves to facilitate a sharing of mutual concerns between families. Relaxed communications within the family are stimulated by the structured recreation time and reinforced through the group discussions. Staff as well as family members gain by the family's appreciation for the child's situation, especially pertaining to institutional procedures. Although there are numerous problems inherent in such a program, the results suggest a need for additional innovative attempts along these same lines.

One possible outcome of this type of visitation program may be the family's realization that they are unable to provide the necessary controls for the child. This conclusion is often at odds with their wish for him to remain in the family. After the family accepts its own limitations, it should be much more open to suggestions for new approaches. In this case, for example, a day-care program such as the one described by Post, Hicks, and Monfort (1968) may be appropriate. The child is kept in the home which avoids the guilt or other feelings accompanying removal. However, during the day the child is engaged in a program at a community center which also allows further work with the family. This type of program is less expensive than institutionalization but is more structured than total release to the family setting.

Another possible finding of family evaluation may be that the child cannot be helped by his own family. If the needs of the child can not be met within the natural family, a foster family may serve the purpose. Witherspoon (1966) described the advantages of foster home placements for juvenile delinquents, particularly when removal of the child from the home community is necessary to interrupt the established chain of delinquency. Special training is of course important for the foster parents as well as counseling to prepare the family to relinquish their legal claims to the child.

Both of the above programs provide alternative modes of action which may be necessary in compensating for some family deficiencies.

THE FUTURE

Despite the growing number of attacks on the family, it probably will continue to exist in its present form for some years. Rather than attacking the family with no productive goals in view, society's energies should be invested in researching the family's effects on delinquency and in modifying existing weaknesses with available resources.

Developing typological approaches to delinquency along dimensions other than social class has proven to be a promising research activity. Similarly, identification of types of families that contribute to delinquent behavior in combination with other factors may prove to be productive. Glueck and Glueck (1970) have combined these two ideas in their latest work with their Social Prediction Scale. They identified three types of delinquents and families from which they come: (1) Core type delinquents who have, among other characteristics, inadequate maternal discipline and no family cohesiveness; (2) Intermediate type delinquents who have some family inadequacies but not as many as the core families; and (3) Failures who came from apparently adequate families. This schema definitely is superficial, especially with regard to recent works on typologies by Quay and his associates (Gerard, Quay and Levinson, 1970) and Warren and her colleagues (Warren, 1969). However, it serves as a beginning in a neglected area of research because it does take directly into account the family's influence on delinquency. Working with the family to effect changes in their behavior has proven to be extremely difficult. Parents seem to be responding to growing criticism of their child-rearing practices by constantly shifting and bending to please the experts or to conform to their child's expressed wishes. Unfortunately, neither society's experts nor their children knows what is best for the family. If nothing else, until answers are available, parents should at least be encouraged to provide a consistent and clear model of what they believe to be appropriate behavior for the child.

REFERENCES

Andry, R. G.: *Delinquency and Parental Pathology.* London, Methuen, 1960.

Bach, G. R.: Father-fantasies and father-typing in father-separated children. *Child Dev, 17:* 63–80, 1946.

Baldwin, A. L., Kalhorn, Joan, and Breese, Fay H.: Patterns of parent behavior. *Psychological Monograph,* 1945, 58 (No. 3).

Bandura, A.: Relationship of family patterns to child behavior disorders. 1960, Stanford Uuniversity, Progress Report M-1734, National Institute of Mental Health.

Bandura, A., Ross, Dorthea and Ross, Sheila: Transmission of aggression through imitation of aggressive models. *J Abnorm Soc Psychol, 63:* 575–582, 1961.

Bandura, A., Ross, D. and Ross Sheila: Imitation of film mediated aggressive models. *J Abnorm Soc Psychol, 66:* 3–11, 1963.

Bandura, A. and Walters, R.: *Adolescent Aggression.* New York, Ronald, 1959.

Becker, W. C., Peterson, D. R., Luria, Zella, Shoemaker, D. J., and Hellmer, L. A.: Relations of factors derived from patient-interview ratings to behavior problems of five-year olds. *Child Dev, 33:* 509–535, 1962.

Becker, W. C., Peterson, D. R., Hellmer, L. A., Shoemaker, D. J., and Quay, H. C.: Factors in parental behavior and personality as related to problem behavior in children. *J Consult Psychol, 23:* 107–110, 1959.

Bender, Lauretta: Psychopathic behavior disorders in children. In R. M. Lindner and R. V. Selinger (Eds.): *Handbook of Correctional Psychology,* New York Philosophical Library, 1947.

Bender, Lauretta: Psychopathic personality disorders in childhood and adolescence, *Arch Crim Psychodynam, 4:* 412–415, 1961.

Bennett, Ivy: *Delinquent and Neurotic Children.* New York, Basic, 1960.

Biller, H. B.: *Father, Child and Sex Role.* Lexington, Mass., Health Lexington Books, 1971.

Brigham, J. C., Rickets, J. L., and Johnson, R. C.: Reported maternal and paternal behaviors of solitary and social delinquents. *J Consult Psychol, 31:* 420–422, 1967.

Burt, C.: *The Young Delinquents.* New York, Appleton, 1929.

Carkhuff, R. R.: Principles of social action in training new careers in human services. *J Counsel Psychol, 18:* 147–151, 1971.

Communications Research Machines Books: *Dexelopmental Psychology Today.* Del Mar, Calif, 1971.

Cooper, D.: *The Death of the Family.* New York, Pantheon, 1970.

Dole, A. A., and Nottingham, J.: Beliefs about human nature held by counseling, clinical and rehabilitation students. *J Counsel Psychol, 16:* 197–202, 1969.

Douvan, E., and Adelson, J.: *The Adolescent Experience.* New York, Wiley, 1966.

Fox, V.: Psychopathy as viewed by a clinical psychologist. *Arch Crim Psychodynam, 4:* 472–479, 1961.

Gerard, R. E., Quay, H. C., and Levinson, R. B.: *Differential treatment: A way to begin.* Washington, D.C., Federal Bureau of Prisons, 1970.

Glueck, S., and Glueck, Eleanor: *Unraveling Juvenile Delinquency.* New York, Commonwealth Fund, 1950.

Glueck, S., and Glueck, Eleanor: *Toward a Typology of Juvenile Offenders: Implications for Therapy and Prevention.* New York, Grune, 1970.

Glueck, S., and Glueck, Eleanor: *Family Environment Delinquency.* Boston, Houghton, 1962.

Greenacre, Phyllis: Conscience in the psychopath. *Am J Orthopsychiatry, 15:* 495–509, 1945.

Harlow, Harry: The heterosexual affectional system in monkeys. *Am Psychol, 17:* 1–9, 1962.

Healy, W. & Bronner, A. L.: *Delinquents and Criminals: Their Making and Unmaking.* New York, Macmillan, 1926.

Hertzog, Elizabeth, and Studia, Cecelia, E.: Fatherless homes: A review of research. *Children,* Sept–Oct, 1968.

Hirsch, I. and Walder, L.: Training mothers in groups as reinforcement therapists for their own children. *Proceedings of the 77th Annual Convention of the American Psychological Association, Washington, D.C.,* 1969, 561–562.

Hoffman, M. L. and Saltzstein, H. D.: Parent discipline and the child's moral development. *J Pers Soc Psychol, 5:* 45–57, 1967.

Jenkins, R. L.: The psychopathic or antisocial personality. *J Nerv Ment Dis, 131:* 318–334, 1960.

Keniston, K.: *Young Radicals.* New York, Harcourt, Brace & World, 1968.

Lipman, H. S.: Psychopathic reactions in children. *Am J Orthopsychiatry, 21:* 227–231, 1961.

Liverant, S.: MMPI differences between parents of disturbed and nondisturbed children. *J Consult Psychol, 23:* 256–260, 1959.

Lym, D. B., and Sawrey, W. L.: The effects of father-absence on Norwegian boys and girls. *J Abnorm Soc Psychol, 59:* 258–262, 1959.

McCandless, B. R.: *Children: Behavior and Development* (2nd ed.) New York, HR & W, 1967.

McCord, W., and McCord, J.: *Psychopathy and Delinquency.* New York, Grune, 1956.

McCord, J. and McCord, W.: The effects of parental role model on criminality. *J Soc Issues, 14:* 66–75, 1958.

McCord, W., McCord, Joan, and Howard, A.: Familial correlates of aggression in nondelinquent male children. *J Abnorm Soc Psychol, 62:* 79–93, 1961.

McCord, Joan, McCord, W., and Howard, A.: Family interaction as antecedent to the direction of male aggressiveness. *J Abnorm Soc Psychol, 66:* 239–242, 1963.

Mead, Margaret: A conversation with Margaret Mead: On the anthropological age. In *Readings in Psychology Today* (2nd ed). Del Mar, Calif., CRM Bks, 1972.

Medinnus, G. R.: Delinquents' perceptions of their parents. *J Consult Psychol, 29:* 592–593, 1965.

Mennel, R. M.: Origins of the juvenile court: Changing perspectives on the legal rights of juvenile delinquents. *Crime Delinq, 18:* 68–78, 1972.

Merrill, Maud A.: *Problems of Child Delinquency.* Boston, 1947.

Miller, W. B.: Lower class culture as a generating milieu of gang delinquency. *J Soc Issues, 14:* 5–19, 1958.

Minuchin, S., Montalvo, B., Guerney, B., Rosman, B., and Schumer, F.: *Families of the Slums.* New York, Basic, 1967.

Mueller, W. J.: Patterns of behavior and their reciprocal impact in the family and in psychotherapy. *J Counsel Psychol, 16:* 2, Pt. 2, 1969.

Patterson, G. R., Cobb, J. A., and Ray, Roberta S.: A social engineering technology for retraining aggressive boys. Paper present for H. Adams and L. Unikel (Eds.)., Georgia Symposium in Experimental Clinical Psychology, Vol. 11., Pergamon Press, 1970.

Patterson, G. R. and Gullion, M. Elizabeth: *Living with Children.* Champaign, Illinois, Research Press, 1968.

Peterson, D. R., and Becker, W. C.: Family interaction and delinquency. In H. C. Quay (Ed.): *Juvenile Delinquency.* New York, D. Van Nostrand, 1965.

Peterson, D. R., Becker, W. C., Hellmer, L. A., Shoemaker, D. J., and Quay, H. C.: Parental attitudes and child adjustment. *Child Dev, 30:* 119–130, 1959.

Pettit, G. A.: *Prisoners of Culture.* New York, Scribner, 1970.

Post, G. C., Hicks, R. A., and Monfort, M. F.: Day-care program for delinquents: A new treatment approach. *Crime and Delinq, 14:* 353–359, 1958.

Reiner, Bernice S., and Kaufman, I.: *Character Disorders in Parents of Delinquents.* New York, Family Service Asso. of America, 1959.

Richardson, H., and Roebuck, J. B.: Minnesota Multiphasic Personality Inventory and California Psychological Inventory differences between delinquents and their nondelinquent siblings. *Proceedings of the 73rd Annual Convention of the American Psychological Association,* Washington, D.C. 1965, 255–256.

Riesman, D.: The young are captives of each other. *Psychol Today,* Oct.: 28–31, 63–67, 1969.

Rubenfeld, S.: *Typological Approaches and Delinquency Control: A Status Report.* Washington, D.C., Department of Health, Education, and Welfare, 1967.

Sears, R., Maccoby, E., and Levin, H.: *Patterns of Child Rearing.* Evanston, Ill., Row, Peterson, 1957.

Shaw, C. R. and McKay, H. D.: *Juvenile Delinquency and Urban Areas,* Chicago, U Chicago P, 1942.

Siegman, A. W.: Father absence during early childhood and antisocial behavior. *J Abnorm Psychol, 71:* 71–74, 1966.

Smith, Judith M. and Smith, D. E. P.: *Child Management.* Ann Arbor, Michigan. Ann Arbor, 1966.

Stark, R., and McEvoy, J., III. Middle-class violence. In *Readings in Psychology Today* (2nd ed.). Del Mar, Calif., CRM, 1972.

Stollery, P. L.: Families come to the institution: A 5-day experience in rehabilitation. *Fed Probation, 34:* 46–53, 1970.

Stolz, Lois M.: *Father Relations of Warborn Children.* Stanford, Calif., Stanford U P, 1954.

Updegraff, Ruth: Recent approaches to the study of the preschool child, III. Influence of parental attitudes upon child behavior. *J Consult Psychol, 3:* 34–36, 1939.

Warren, Marguerite Q.: The case for differential treatment of delinquents. *Ann Am Acad Poli Soc Sci, 381:* 47–59, 1969.

Williams, P.: School dropouts. *NEA, 52:* 10–12, 1963.

Witherspoon, A. W.: Foster home placements for juvenile delinquents. *Fed Probation, 30:* 48–52, 1966.

Wood, B. S., Wilson, G. G., Jessor, R., and Bogan, R. B.: Trouble-shooting behavior in a correctional institution: Relationship to inmates' definition of their situation. *Am J Orthopsychiatry, 36:* 795–802, 1966.

CHAPTER 7

FAMILY CRISIS INTERVENTION

ROBERTA E. MALOUF AND JAMES F. ALEXANDER

●●

PHILOSOPHY

TRAINING

TECHNIQUES

●●

T HIS MATERIAL will describe the basic elements of the short term family crisis therapy approach which we have developed for treating families of delinquent teenagers (Alexander and Parsons, 1973; Parsons and Alexander, 1973). In keeping with the purposes of this chapter, three aspects of the program will be highlighted: underlying philosophy, training and supervision models, and the main techniques utilized. Prior to covering these issues, however, it must be emphasized that one important aspect of any program development is the utilization of both process and outcome research designs to evaluate program impact. However, as this issue is well covered in both the subsequent presentation* and the two research papers mentioned above, it will not be pursued here except to emphasize that evaluation is not an alternative but a requisite in any treatment endeavor.

---

* Alexander, J. F.: *Choice points, dilemmas, and polemics.* Paper presented at the National Conference on Training in Family Therapy, sponsored by the Philadelphia Child Guidance Clinic, Philadelphia, November, 1972.

PHILOSOPHY

With increasing demands for service from community members, helping agencies (ranging from community mental health centers to school psychological services) are seriously considering the feasibility of short term crisis therapy as a treatment of choice in many instances. For example, in developing the techniques for reducing "soft" delinquency (e.g., runaway, ungovernable, truancy, soft drug use, repeated curfew violations, etc.) in the program described here, several considerations were incorporated. At the most pragmatic level, delinquents and their families typically represent a poorly motivated population with only one-third to one-half of the cases completing counseling programs. While the often-heard explanations for this phenomenon (e.g., low motivation, subcultural values antagonistic to counseling, etc.) are probably true, the present program assumed that the responsibility for motivation rests with the treatment agency, not the clients. For this treatment population, then, change techniques had to be understandable, direct, rapid, and, probably most important, produce hope for benefit to *all* family members. Programs giving the message that delinquents should change *for the sake of their parents* or vice-versa, have, at best, a long uphill fight to face.

This emphasis on the importance of change or benefit for all family members reflects a second premise, that the understanding and potential change in an individual's behavior is impossible and even meaningless without knowledge of the interpersonal system or systems which influence that individual. This interpersonal systems model emphasizes that an explanation as to why a behavior does or does not occur lies entirely in the kinds of responses it elicits from other members of the system. All behaviors are seen as serving some communicative function within a particular system, in that they elicit certain responses from other members of that system and thus maintain established roles and relationships. It follows, then, that if the function of given problem responses is changed and alternate ways of eliciting desired payoffs are discovered and emitted, the problem behaviors are less likely to reoccur. However, because problem behaviors cannot occur in isolation from the system, it is also important to involve all system members (i.e., the family) in identifying how each member is helping to maintain problem behaviors and in generating alternate social maneuvers for each person. The goal of the therapy program becomes the involvement of all family members in their joint responsibility for compromise and change in order to meet and cope with whatever problems arise. This goal stands in contrast to many crisis models in which the goal of therapy interventions is to return family members to some precrisis state of equilibrium. Such a concept, precrisis equilibrium, is not appropriate in families of teenagers who, almost by definition, are undergoing natural, developmental role changes. Thus in contrast to behavior modification programs with preadolescents, the goal of this program is not to modify specific behaviors (e.g., school attendance) but to train the family in effective problem solving techniques to adaptively meet the changes inevitably occurring in adolescence. Specific maladaptive behaviors are seen as interpersonal strategies designed to influence the system in certain ways. For example, failing school may represent a way of maintaining separateness in an upwardly mobile middle-class family which places great importance on success in school, but, in this case, would not be the treatment focus per se. Instead attention would be focused on the development of alternative strategies for maintaining separateness, which at the same time would not include the maladaptive or "get nowhere" aspects of failure in school.

This example incorporates the third major premise of the program, that of changing strategies, not functions or people. In a short term context, it is unrealistic to think of changing "personalities" or "needs." A wife, for example, who "needs" a more involved husband and uses her daughter's delinquent behavior to force him to assume more paternal responsibility, will not easily become an autonomous individual. However, it may be possible to replace the delinquency with more acceptable behaviors that still function to elicit father's attention and thus continue to meet mother's need Of course, in this case father and daughter also have "needs," and a similar functional analysis must be made for them. The main point, however, is that therapy is aimed at changing strategies to meet needs, not the needs themselves.

Inextricably bound to the issue of system membership is a rationale for seeing families as opposed to individuals. Regardless of the unit of focus in therapy, the therapist, and often his agency, automatically acquires membership in the individual's social milieu. It is in this fact that defining the family as the unit of therapeutic interest has great appeal. First, it is a more efficient use of time and energy. When working with a client on a one-to-one basis, the therapist has many significant others with whom he must deal *in absentia*. In dealing with families, a therapist has a vital, functioning system with which to work. He can watch a family in action, thereby collecting more reliable samples of behavior than if one member described his family, and he can provide a setting in which the family can practice ways of interacting that can be used in natural settings. While individuals can practice new styles too, there is less chance that newly learned responses will generalize and, better yet, be maintained in a system in which other members have not had an opportunity to deliberately select new maneuvers as well.

A second and, perhaps, even more important advantage of a family rather than an individual focus is the reduced likelihood that a therapist-client-family triangle will emerge. This sort of triangle can easily become a miniature family in which few clear communications are exchanged. Therapists, like family members, are social people who find themselves devoting time and energy to produce changes which are only sabotaged by a "malevolent" family. This situation generates blame and fault finding, both of which are incompatible with change. In seeing the client and his significant others, however, the therapist's behavior must be the embodiment of the statement that to help the individual client is to help the entire family. Working with the entire family helps the therapist to disengage from faultfinding and blaming of any single family member and, instead, to appreciate the symbiotic nature of the system and the fact that the pathology lies, not with the individual, but with the interactions among individuals.

TRAINING

Training of new and, in our project, relatively inexperienced therapists followed many of the principles utilized in the treatment program itself. The first experience is in group meetings, where trainees are introduced to the fundamentals of the interpersonal systems model, given copies of the training manual, and presented with training videotapes which highlight family and therapist behaviors and roles in terms of the functions they serve within the system. In these early sessions it is emphasized that minute-to-minute communications are of primary importance, and historical data are important only to confirm or reject hypotheses as to consistent family relationships. To emphasize the functional basis of the systems approach, examples are demonstrated where therapist behaviors elicit and maintain family resistance in spite of the best intentions behind his "guidance." This principle is extended to the families themselves, where the functional impact of behavior may be quite different from what was "apparently" intended by the initiator. This point cannot be overemphasized, as trainees experience great difficulty in not identifying some family members as the malevolent persecutors, and others as the innocent victims.

The early didactic training phase is soon replaced by live observations, via one-way mirrors, of therapists seeing families. Whenever possible, trainees first observe one of the project supervisors seeing a family with another supervisor behind the one-way mirrors providing minute-to-minute translations of the interactions, identifying successful maneuvers, dead-ends, and idiosyncratic styles of the therapist. Trainees also observe sessions of other trainees, and after all sessions, group discussions are held to plan alternative strategies, discuss productive and counterproductive therapist maneuvers, role play difficult situations, etc. After four to five weeks in this passive role, trainees begin seeing families, usually with a more experienced therapist at first. As before, direct supervision by supervisors and other trainees continues as do the follow-up group discussions.

In summary, trainees receive much the same experience as do the families they will see: feedback is immediate, modeling and role playing are utilized to change and practice new behaviors, therapists and families are conceptualized as a system in order to eliminate blaming when interactions become unproductive, and the determinants of behaviors are defined in terms of their consequences, not their "intent" or "cause."

TECHNIQUES

Labeling. A major technique involving three facets is that of labeling. In this process the therapist identifies or asks each family member to identify the sequence of events that lead to a particular event (in or out of the session). In doing so, the therapist slows the pace of interaction and generates a clearer sequential picture of events, including the part *all* family members played in the sequence (for example, it is often impactful to point out that a particular sequence occurred in the absence of a family member; so that member may have played an important part by being absent!). The labeling also sets a stage for subsequent cause-and-effect interpretations which serve to emphasize that more than one family member is necessary for any one behavior sequence to occur or not occur. From this point, families are often more willing to see these cause-and-effect chains as modifiable and to develop alternatives early in the chain.

A second facet of the labeling process is the discovery of inevitable differences in perception and interpretation of events. When it becomes clear that family members perceive the same event in different ways, the therapist can move to the important process of training the family in clear communication and feedback. Such clarity is basic to the process of reciprocal contracting (*see* below).

The third benefit from labeling is that it allows the therapist to avoid blaming. Family members are seen as "trapped" in a sequence of events that have certain functions, and no one alone is at fault. Family members, of course, tend to resist this nonblaming maneuver (e.g., "But if he would only . . ."). However, this noncritical labeling process does set the stage for further negotiation and reciprocal contracting.

Reciprocal contracting. The second and perhaps most important technique in the therapy program is the negotiation of explicit and reciprocal contracts. While the purpose of labeling is to make explicit the patterns of cause-effect relationships that exist within the family system, it is the process of reciprocal contracting that helps the family to jointly develop alternative response patterns. The guiding principle of reciprocal contracting is that the contract must offer some payoff for all involved parties. After each family member is asked for his version of the painful events, the family is asked if the problem they had just described is something they want to change and what could (not would) they change. After the range of possible alternatives is discussed, each family member is asked to make a change, *but only in return* for a reciprocal change in another family member (e.g., son attends school if father allows him to use the car on weekends, and vice versa). It is important also to emphasize that all family members must negotiate contracts (mother-father, father-mother, etc.), not just the obvious troublesome dyads, such as mother-child or father-child. This point distinguishes the program from many behavior modification approaches, as the focus is on mutual problem solving (i.e., negotiation for reciprocal contracts) in the family as a whole, not just the elimination of specific target behaviors. In guiding these negotiations, the therapist can insure that the new contracts serve to replace the functions formerly served by delinquent behavior. In our prior example of mother's need to keep father involved, she can agree to stop nagging daughter (daughter's request) only in return for father's agreeing to check school attendance (meeting mother's need for involvement). He, in turn, can agree to do so only if allowed to go fishing alone on Saturday, meeting his request to be away from the family at times.

When practicing the art of reciprocal contracting, therapists have several means of determining the likelihood that a contract will be maintained. First the therapist should ask himself the question, "Why should I follow through if I were that person? What is the payoff, and is it reinforcing for the individual?" Second, the therapist should ask each family member these same questions. Hearing each member describe his payoff tells the therapist how reciprocal the contract is and therefore gives him some idea of how well it will work. For example, if a mother answers, "My reward will be seeing my son be a better person because good boys come home on time," the therapist knows this mother has not yet appreciated the importance of her behavior in the system and the fact that she has needs for herself personally, not just in terms of her son. A reciprocal contract has not been made until each member can describe what he personally will receive if he helps to maintain the contract. An acceptable response from our reluctant mother might be, "When he doesn't break curfew, I don't have to get out of bed in the middle of the night to let him in the house," or "I won't have to listen to him and his dad fight the next morning and then get a headache."

Focus on the marriage. Of considerable importance, representing more of a point of emphasis than a specific therapy technique, is the focus on the parents as a special problem solving unit. As implied in the above discussion, it is crucial that the marital dyad receive special attention apart from the children. The goal in stressing the need for parents to directly struggle and cooperate with each other is twofold. First, it serves to remove the children from a middleman position in the marriage so that they no longer have responsibility for keeping the married pair together or apart, and, second, it reminds parents that parenting is a job that requires both of them to be involved directly with each other in resolving problems. In focusing on parents as a married couple, the therapist steers contract negotiation to include a necessary contract between parents. This does not mean the parents are asked to no longer disagree with each other, but rather to agree or disagree directly with each other rather than through children. For example, a father may want his son to attend church three times a week, but mother disagrees with this. Nevertheless father expects and demands that mother enforce his rule with son. A goal for therapy would be to remove son from this marital conflict by creating a contract in which father must enforce his own rules with son and agree to disagree with his wife as to the moral value of church meetings for their son, i.e., let them agree or disagree but without son.

In summary, just as the training model emphasized feedback and practice of specific therapy techniques, the therapy model stresses the importance of providing a setting for families in which they can observe and participate in the process of clarification of ongoing communications and the deliberate selection of alternative responses to each other. It is stressed that the process of labeling and reciprocal contracting are skills that the family can use when problems arise and are not a magic that "good" families have and "bad" families lack. The attention given to the parents serves to bring into focus for the entire family the fact that parents have, not only special responsibilities, but also a unique relationship, and that this relationship, within the context of children, requires direct communications and problem solving.

REFERENCES

Alexander, J. F.: Defensive and supportive communications in normal and deviant families. *Journal of Consulting and Clinical Psychology, 40:* 223–231, 1973.

Alexander, J. F. and Parsons, B. V.: Short term behavioral intervention with delinquent families: Impact on process and recidivism. *Journal of Abnormal Psychology,* 1973 (in press).

Bergin, A. E.: The evaluation of therapeutic outcomes. In Bergin, A. E. and Garfield, S. L. (Eds.): *Handbook of psychotherapy and behavior change: An empirical analysis.* New York, Wiley, 1970.

Haley, J.: *Changing families: A family therapy reader.* New York, Grune and Stratton, 1971.

Parad, H. J. and Caplan, G.: A framework for studying families in crisis. In Parad, H. J. (Ed.): *Crisis intervention: Selected readings.* New York, Family Service Association of America, 1965.

Parsons, B. V. and Alexander, J. F.: Short term family intervention: A therapy outcome study. *Journal of Consulting and Clinical Psychology,* 1973 (in press).

Strupp, H. H.: *Psychotherapy and the modification of abnormal behavior.* New York, McGraw-Hill, 1971.

Watzlawick, P., Beavin, J. H. and Jackson, D. D.: *Pragmatics of human communication.* New York, Norton, 1967.

CHAPTER 8

MULTIPLE IMPACT THERAPY WITH FAMILIES: CURRENT PRACTICAL APPLICATIONS

ALBERTO C. SERRANO

•••

•••

BRIEF BACKGROUND OF THE METHOD

THIS CHAPTER WILL describe current applications of a family-centered treatment approach that was developed as Multiple Impact Therapy (McGregor, Ritchie, Serrano, Schuster, Goolishian, and McDanald, 1964) at the University of Texas Medical Branch in Galveston, Texas. The MIT project, which studied fifty-five families of disturbed adolescents over a four-year period (1958–62), involved the use of a brief intensive treatment technique, in which an orthopsychiatric team met with the family of an emotionally disturbed adolescent during two consecutive days, and included team-family sessions and individual and group interviews with various combinations of team and family members. Its purpose was to study the brief-therapy approach departing from the usual once-a-week format and to attempt to use the cumulative impact and convergence of mental health professionals and family members, meeting within a two-day period, to enhance natural healing processes. We had earlier observed that families, threatened with serious emotional and/or behavioral disturbance in a child, often traveled long distances to the University of Texas Medical Branch in Galveston to consult the Youth Development Project, an outpatient psychiatric clinic for adolescents. We found, as did Gerald Caplan (1956), that the crisis, not only facilitated the engagement of the family in seeking help, but also opened the way to self-rehabilitating family processes with brief therapeutic intervention. Most of the techniques used in the MIT project had been reported by other group and family therapists separately; Peck (1953); Johnson (1953); Whitaker *et al.* (1949); and Ackerman (1958). The design included the use of multiple therapists in individual and group situations with the family members, often inviting relevant community representatives as conveners.

Follow up studies, that were routine at six and eighteen months, indicate that the treatment results were comparable to more intensive long-term therapies. In forty-three of the fifty-five cases treated during the first two years of the project, family self-rehabilitative processes remained effectively mobilized. In seven families the presenting problem was unchanged or worse. The impact of the technique was indicated by the fact that twenty-eight of the cases had continued toward self-rehabilitation after only the minimal procedure. Fifteen cases required more attention and led to longer term team-family centered work. This was particularly needed in cases of extreme psychopathology. This led us to develop more flexible applications of the basic design after the project was completed. Encouraging results were obtained with psychotic or near psychotic cases where the procedure was repeated every four to six weeks through the first year. We also found that intervention at the time of intense crises with a stable and functional family responded favorably with one-day or even half-day intake procedure resembling the first day of MIT followed by brief follow up visits.

THE FAMILY-THERAPY PROGRAM IN SAN ANTONIO

For the past several years, I have been in San Antonio, Texas as Director of a private non-profit outpatient mental health clinic for children, adolescents and their families. The Community Guidance Center of Bexar County is affiliated with the University of Texas Medical School at San Antonio and serves a city-county of close to one million population that includes about 51 percent Mexican-Americans, 42 percent Anglos and 7 percent Blacks. The Center has a community mental health orientation and uses an ecological social-systems approach to the understanding and the treatment of emotional, behavioral, and learning disorders (Auerswald, 1972). Service and training run close together. The program underlines the importance of the family and of other significant social systems, such as school, in the evaluation and treatment. All cases are assessed on a family-centered basis, with emphasis placed on short-term therapies including family and group treatment modalities. Those cases needing residential or day-care treatment are referred to the San Antonio Children's Center, a psychiatric non-profit mental health agency to which we are closely related through sharing staff and through joint affiliation with the University of Texas Medical School at San Antonio. It also has a family-centered philosophy. Let us examine now our population served and the manner in which the original MIT techniques have been adapted.

THE REFERRAL NETWORK

In our program most referrals arise from schools, family and friends, medical practitioners, and social agencies. They represent all socioeconomic and ethnic groups in close proportion to the Bexar County population. We find it essential to "think family" while working with other social systems, notably schools, health and social agencies, churches, and neighborhood centers. Caregivers of those systems are of crucial value as conveners of troubled families to get help from our staff. We often invite those community representatives for diagnostic work, planning, treatment, follow-up and further care. The use of an ecological approach, involving other systems around the troubled family, facilitates a clearer, more dynamic understanding of what appears pathological, while concurrently assessing existing strengths and evoking self-rehabilitative processes. Including other systems in our work also teaches the families to negotiate with them more effectively and to attempt to change dysfunctional systems.

Priming a case at the referral level is of great importance. For example: how a principal of a school presents his referral to us to the family is often more important than what we say or do at the time of initial contact. Thus, personally knowing the sources of referral and having shared respect and understanding for our different yet overlapping professional tasks greatly facilitate a relevant referral, with a family more willing to engage in therapeutic work, less prone to feel rejected or coerced by the referring agent. The family then will view our intervention as assistance to them, rather than us as persecution or judgment.

THE INITIAL CONTACT

Typically an intake worker, who is a mental health paraprofessional, is the first person to respond to the initial telephone call or the walk-in visit. The worker takes the initial referral data, explains the services available through the center, and explains the need to meet with all family members—typically, all those living at home and, frequently, other significant relatives. Considerable effort is applied to invite fathers who often receive a personal call to explain the significance of their presence; we suggest this be done preferably by a male staff member of the same ethnic group. The father is invited to attend at least the initial evaluation session. Very often a reputedly uncooperative father comes willing to participate, as a new authority is being defined for his role. The intake worker also may discuss the possible inclusion of a referring source as convener. A developmental questionnaire and forms for reports from the family physician and from the school are mailed to obtain further collateral information. That we have a charge on a sliding fee scale according to income is also brought up, although the actual fee is set later.

PREPARATION FOR EVALUATION

If the problem is an emergency or a crisis, the family may be seen on the same day or so without waiting for reports. Most cases, however, are regularly scheduled and are seen within one to four weeks, depending on the volume of service at the time, and will come prepared to stay for two to three hours of initial evaluation.

For a best possible match with staff and trainees, the team to work with a particular family is assigned, preferably, by taking under consideration several factors: nature and severity of symptoms; sex and age; and racial, cultural and religious background. We have to take under consideration that a team may include child psychiatrists, psychologists, social workers, educational specialists, mental health paraprofessionals, medical students, child psychiatry fellows, psychiatry, psychology and pediatric residents, social work students, and pastoral counseling and mental health worker trainees.

In making an ideal assignment, it is very useful to match the family with a team ready to "speak the language" of the family. The use of paraprofessionals facilitates the engagement of the family, while professionals provide specific clinical competence to the diagnostic process. Considerable effort is required to reconfirm appointments with clients and to notify referral sources of these in order to minimize the non-shows and cancellations.

THE TEAM

One or two staff members of different disciplines are typically included along with one or two trainees and, when available, the family convener. They review the existing material for about fifteen minutes and discuss possible hypotheses and strategies, including tentative plans as to which team member will go with what division of the family when the separate sessions start. The more senior member of the team most frequently will lead the group and act as "live supervisor." Those new to the method are encouraged to be active, for the ideal multiple therapy situation calls for active participation, rather than for passive observation. Thus the ideal multiple therapy situation presents a smooth collaboration between the team members and provides a model for identification for the family members, who often will then experience that it is possible for adults to communicate openly and respectfully. Excessive politeness, on one hand, and competitiveness, on the other, tend to interfere with the efficiency of the team intervention and greatly reduces its impact as a diagnostic and therapeutic agent. The proper climate is fostered by the senior therapist in the team who demonstrates, by example, the benefits of a team collaborating as an open system. Those who criticize the use of multiple therapy underline the difficulties of teaming up professionals. We have found that merely grouping a team, as an administrative decision, is often ineffective or disastrous or may end as a polite "low key" treatment intervention. Self-selection and the opportunity to openly discuss the development of the relationship with each other, along with supervision and consultation, is, in our experience, most effective in facilitating a climate of openness and growth. As the co-therapist relationship grows, the therapists become more sensitive and responsive to the families.

There are two major functions that explain and justify the

use of more than one therapists; one deals with specific treatment advantages and the other concerns the training of and consulting with psychotherapists. The complexities of treating more than one individual, as it is in the treatment of couples, families and groups, make it extremely difficult and taxing for a single therapist to take on. The understanding and management of the multiple transferential problems is rather complex, if at all accessible to one therapist's awareness. The co-therapy situation provides a "stereoscopic view" of the family and lends opportunity to the treatment twosome for a division of labor in which they may involve themselves at different levels, such as in a tennis match, where one plays in front while the other covers the back, enjoying enough flexibility so that they can alternate in their roles. The co-therapists also monitor each other and, in so doing, provide a growth model for themselves and for the group under treatment. Furthermore, the co-therapy model more effectively deals with the multiple transference problems encountered in treating families. It is also of special value for children and adolescents to witness adults who are able to deal openly and honestly with their agreements and disagreements and who promote a climate of respect and comradeship. As Whitaker and Napier (1972) said, the co-therapist "acts as a triangulating agent between the other therapist and the family." Also, since there can be a problem when the trainee tries to imitate and depend too much on his teacher's style and philosophy, we find it very important that trainees get a chance to work in co-therapy with different therapists, to experience other styles, and to learn about how senior therapists deal with feelings, beyond knowing of their intellectual abilities and technical skills.

INITIAL TEAM-FAMILY SESSION

After a brief social phase of welcome and introductions (at which time permission may be requested for one-way mirror observation or video taping), the family members are invited to describe in their own words what they see as their problem. An effort is made soon to give each member an opportunity to give his perspective of the situation.

It is frequent that, at the initial team-family conference, the family reports some degree of improvement since the referral contact and voices concern over the need for further evaluation. This is typical resistance aimed at blocking further study by the team. Other families are critical and uncomfortable about open discussion of problems in front of the children. We recognize their discomfort and assure them that observation of their patterns of communications is an essential part of the team's work and that they will have an opportunity to discuss more private matters in separate sessions. After an initial reluctance, most families open up and start defining problem areas. Participating siblings and significant members of the extended family often reveal crucial material. Discrepancies, incongruencies, or new historical data soon bring new light into the referring problem. Little effort is made at this point to extend the focus of intervention beyond the family's level of readiness to engage with the team in the helping process. Since the family, typically, came because one of their children presents behavioral, emotional, and/or learning difficulties, it may want help just for that. Side-taking, confrontation, and interpretations are reserved for later in most cases. Respect for the gradual unfolding of historical material as the result of the growing process of team-family interaction, in place of attempts to obtain a formal chronological history, is also essential. It is our experience that low-middle-class families expect us to be more direct, supportive, active, and goal-oriented than upper-middle-class families, regardless of ethnic background. As other problem areas start emerging before the team, their intervention should reflect respect, concern, openness, curiosity, and some humor, but never at the family's expense. Team members become mediators, go-betweens, and help bridge communication between family members. This is demonstrated as team members check with each other and share impressions and feelings. This is particularly useful when a community representative is present as convener who has the trust of the family from earlier contacts. The initial team-family session generally lasts about forty-five minutes to one hour, by which time problem areas are more clearly defined and tension is sufficiently mobilized to facilitate considerable catharsis in the separate and individual sessions.

SEPARATE SESSIONS

We regularly see the referred patient in an individual interview that later may be scheduled for further psychiatric, psychological or psycho-educational evaluation. Most often this interview is conducted by psychiatric or psychology staff for the purpose of formal diagnostic documentation. Interviews with parents and siblings, and other separate conferences for any boundary consideration are typically held according to family structure and the team's impressions. Often it is useful to see siblings together before seeing the nominal patient in a separate interview. We try to convey the attitude that while we deal initially with the symptoms presented by one family member, we are also concerned with the family structure and functioning as a whole, just as we are concerned with each individual member's functioning and feelings. We believe, that to understand the family as a whole and its interpersonal transactions, that include dyads, triads, and coalitions, the significance of the individual should not be overlooked. Furthermore, it is essential to perceive the family in its ecological social context.

Separate conferences are run concurrently and for about thirty to forty-five minutes. It is possible for an interviewer to leave a session to join another when there is something to be checked out or shared. The overlapping interview is an important contribution of the original MIT design and offers an unusual opportunity for developing more open communication within the family, between team and family, and within the team. An outstanding feature of the overlapping interview can be seen in the summary given by the therapist to the oncoming team member. His review, not only informs the visiting therapist of the content and progress of the session, but also conveys to the patient the therapist's understanding of what the patient feels and thinks.

Some general interpretations can be offered, describing certain family styles, congruencies, and incongruencies in a tactful way. The therapist encourages the patient to correct or enlarge the summary, thus minimizing any pretense of infallibility. The incoming therapist in turn shares information or impressions gained from other family members. It is essential to keep a careful balance between honesty and tact, by selecting information to be shared in a way that it will bridge communication gaps rather than destroy trust in the therapists or create further family splits. The discretion and clinical judgment of the more experienced team member will provide a model for the more junior members to follow. In the separate, as well as in the overlapping sessions, some of the existing resources are explored and plans for further evaluation, planning, or treatment begin to emerge.

FINAL TEAM-FAMILY SESSION

Frequently team members conduct a brief conference without the family before the final team-family session. Convergence develops with the integration of information gathered from various sessions, along with the intake data and reports from referring sources, school and family physician. In sharing impressions, feelings, and recommendations, it is typical for the less experienced team members to be overwhelmed by the overload of information obtained verbally and nonverbally in their contracts with the family. They regularly get "sucked into" the powerful dynamic forces of the family and identify themselves with different members, typically with the symptomatic youth, who may be seen as a powerless victim of vicious parental or social forces. Indeed it is not uncommon that the entire team mirrors family dysfunctional interaction until they themselves become aware of it or a supervisor interprets and helps them recognize the pattern. This "gut awareness" is most useful to really understand how the dynamic equilibrium of the family affects all its members. We have to also underline how the index patient contributes through deviant behaviors to the maintenance of the disturbed equilibrium.

Finding ways of negotiating change through family members, who are willing to break the now predictable patterns, is one of the major tasks of the diagnostic team, as the assessment of their readiness and willingness to change is crucial before moving into family therapy per se. Strengths and weaknesses in the family structure and in the function of its members are more clearly understood. The referral symptoms start making sense. Scapegoating mechanisms are more obvious. Often it becomes evident to key family members that the initial contract in which they brought one individual to be changed is now inappropriate. This awareness evokes feelings of depression and guilt, with family members taking turns at blaming themselves. The significance of historical and environmental factors acquires a better perspective.

I have come to prefer having the team conference in which we discuss diagnostic impressions and management plans in front of the family. We agree with Whitaker and Napier (1972) in that with this way we become more tactful and honest. The use of jargon becomes irrelevant and, as professionals, we are forced to describe pathology with respect and simplicity. I am always impressed with the attentiveness of the family and how they appreciate our sharing with them our feelings and reasoning. I do not think this approach is indicated when the evaluation process is far from reaching closure or when team members have serious divergences that may not be explained merely on countertransferential terms. Teams or small groups have family-like qualities and may be dysfunctional, not just because they are replicating or amplifying family pathology. The use of supervisors and consultants minimizes the possible deleterious impact of a "disturbed" team. In our long experience, the advantages of the use of teams far outweigh the occasional difficulties because, in most cases, there is a high degree of convergence among team members.

After participating for over two hours of significant interaction with the team, the family members have typically experienced a new awareness of their difficulties in the climate of respect, honesty, and openness presented to them. The symptoms they brought to our attention have become more understandable and are frequently "owned" by several or by most family members. This does not apply of course to those cases where a key family member suppresses essential information, carries a hidden agenda not uncovered until the end, or engages in dishonest manipulations while intimidating other family members. Then the cautious use of confrontation and interpretation is indicated in order to precipitate a crisis scene of therapeutic value. This requires good timing and considerable self-awareness by the therapist to minimize victimizing family members in a power struggle. A therapist, who is unclear about the boundaries of his role and of his authority, may misrepresent as therapeutic confrontation what in reality is the acting out of his power fantasies. This session concludes with the planning for further specialized psychiatric, psychological, neurological, psychoeducational, and/or further family evaluation. In a large number of cases it is possible to move into a family therapy program and contract for a limited number of team-family therapy sessions, averaging six to ten spaced weekly or biweekly for one to one and a half hours. Frequently we like to combine several individual sessions and/or group therapy and/or placement in our educo-therapy program in the overall plan.

A final team debriefing takes place shortly after the family leaves. This serves the purpose of clarification of team interaction and family and individual dynamics with senior consultants, including the planning for further diagnostic work, treatment, or disposition. Consultants are typically available in all evaluations.

In about 30 percent of the cases seen, a pattern, offering one or two sessions and including recommendations to other agencies is found adequate. Following the initial team-family evaluation, we see in those cases enough evidence of impact and of self-rehabilitative processes on the way. A follow up in one to two months is scheduled, at which time, most often, progress has been established and the goals of the family and of the referring source have been met. The team remains available to the family for further consultation as needed.

In about 20 percent of the cases, further care and follow up is handled by the community representatives that functioned as conveners of a family under their care. Typically this involves mental health professionals and paraprofessionals from other centers, school counselors, juvenile officers, clergymen, and welfare workers. In such cases the team-family evaluation has provided consultation and training to the convener in addition to primary care of the family.

MOVING INTO FAMILY THERAPY

When we move from team-family evaluation to a family-therapy phase a smaller team is quite adequate and a co-therapy twosome provides a good balance. In most cases the co-therapists participated in the evaluation process, thereby facilitating continuity of care and rapport with the family. Larger teams are needed only where an extended family network is involved. The average course of family therapy involves six to ten sessions, frequently on a weekly basis during the early phase, followed by meetings spaced every two weeks or more. To help the family experience change and growth by itself, dependency must be minimized. Maximum effort to help each family member assume responsibility for personal change must be made, as, for instance, the designing of homework which will not be controlled by others for its success or failure. This facilitates the redefinition of self-boundaries and the feeling of being in command as individuals. Such experiences frequently break the interlocking dysfunctional equilibrium and open new avenues of more functional interaction and respect between family members. Often the homework looks to them insignificant, unacceptable, or even detrimental to another member of the family. A case in point is the mother who is afraid of disturbing her child who regularly intrudes while she is in the bathroom. Once she decides to experiment locking the door and setting a clear boundary for her privacy, she experiences great relief after some initial distress. Or there is the father who regularly jumps his son for behaving provocatively toward his mother and later is constantly reprimanded by his wife for not showing love to his son. He choses to experiment, giving himself five minutes before taking the "bait." He reports that he enjoyed the feeling of mastery which he experienced with new understanding and perspective. Or there is the young man who expects his father to deny him privileges and who presents his requests in anger or with poor timing. Aware-ness of the self-defeating pattern allows him to try as home-work to schedule sufficient time with his parents to bargain for permission to take a demanding summer job away from home. He was impressed with how well they listened and responded to the factual information he presented without anger or pressure.

The fact that successes are achieved and "owned" by each member greatly facilitates descapegoating and stops the mutual blaming which tends to slow down or arrest the natural growth potential of a stable and functional family system.

Let me emphasize again the need for flexibility which, in the context of a family-centered treatment program, makes it possible to include individual therapy for one of more members, medication, group therapy, a referral for special education placement, vocational rehabilitation, day-care or residential treatment.

As their defensive patterns are modified, families frequently experience more discomfort and present resistance to further intervention. They may close ranks, defending themselves and perceiving the team as an enemy. Other times they may try to seduce the therapists with premature leaps into health (Zuk, 1971). The family is experiencing new awareness that brings out fear, excitement, sadness, anger, confusion, and ulti-mate joy. Respect for their strengths, conveyed by the team, allows them to unfold their healthy resources while recognizing what is pathological and dysfunctional. Redefinition of roles and clarification of generational boundaries, of patterns of inter-action, and of communication also facilitates a rapid process of self-rehabilitation.

Long term team-family therapy is, in our experience, as an outpatient program, less feasible because of the time commit-ment required from family members and because of other clin-ical considerations. When indicated it involves a seriously dis-turbed member, typically a psychotic or borderline psychotic youth which requires treatment over an extended period of time. In most cases, we maintain a family-centered orientation, focusing on one or two of the more available family members in individual, conjoint or group therapy, including occasional sessions with the whole family, particularly at the time of crises, extended vacations or termination.

TERMINATION

Termination is planned from the very first as treatment goals are established and strengths are assessed. It has been our experience that working through is done by the family members in the real world and not in the therapists office. Because dependency is not fostered, families learn to rely on their own strengths. I do not want to convey the impression that family therapy solves all mental health troubles. "Thinking family" provides an excellent perspective of the pathological and of the healthy forces in the ecosystem of individuals. Proficiency in other treatment modalities by the therapists, as well as knowledge of existing community resources, is a must. Training should also provide for the healthy recognition that some families, unwilling to change, are untreatable. However, even in those cases, a family orientation can be used to minimize the negative impact of a chaotic or an oppressive family, by carefully developing and maintaining a therapeutic alliance with key members while a more individualized treatment approach is offered to those willing to change.

We find that team-family therapy makes the termination process easier. Perhaps it is less conflicting for families to leave the therapist when he is not alone, not unlike the adolescent experiencing less conflict if he goes away from home leaving two parents that have a good relationship to support each other.

FAMILY THERAPY WITH ADOLESCENTS

Another application of co-therapy answers the argument frequently used to avoid involving the adolescents with their families. The reasoning explains that developmentally the adolescent tries to separate himself from the family, sharpens his sense of identity, and moves away from them physically and emotionally. We find that most of the adolescents who come to our attention have unclear self-boundaries. Family assessment and family treatment helps them clarify these boundaries and often redefines their identity in the context of their family. The use of a team provides more neutral areas for the adolescent and his family to relate to. Frequently one of the therapists may then be more polarized in the direction of the parents while another is able to develop a closer understanding of the adolescent. It is also possible to split the family to provide separate interviews at one time or another for different members including siblings and members of the extended family.

SOME FINAL THOUGHTS

We find it most helpful to think in terms of ecological social systems within the format of the team-family-centered technology. The complexities of understanding emotional, behavioral, and learning disorders cannot be explained by one simple theoretical model or etiology. It is unlikely that one professional will ever have all the knowledge and the technical expertise needed to integrate all the items of information surrounding the presenting symptoms. The traditional use of an orthopsychiatric team, studying a case separately, frequently fails to integrate theoretical concepts or to explain how disturbed symptoms emerge. To study those symptoms in isolation is to ignore that they appear in a social framework and that they are relevant only in the ecological context in which they appear. The team-family model offers us an ideal approach to the evaluation and the treatment of emotional disorders with an ecological systems philosophy.

These current adaptations of the multiple impact therapy approach also facilitates the use of wider treatment possibilities, notably combining therapies to include individual, couples, group, family and network techniques, in as much as the therapists do not need to participate conjointly in all treatment modalities.

A most useful aspect of the use of team-family therapy relates to the case with which additional professionals and trainees can become members of the team (Serrano, 1973). We regularly incorporate medical students, during their brief psychiatric clerkship, to get exposed to the ecological aspects of mental and emotional illness. Their rotation has consistently been reported as one of the most exciting and relevant psychiatric learning experiences they had. Quoting a recent graduate, "there is where psychiatry is at."

REFERENCES

Ackerman, N. W.: The psychodynamics of family life. *Diagnosis and Treatment of Family Relationships.* New York, Basic, 1958.

Auerswald, E. H.: Interdisciplinary versus ecological approach. In Sager and Kaplan: *Progress in Group and Family Therapy.* New York, Brunner-Mazel, 309–321, 1972.

Caplan, G.: An approach to the study of the family mental health. *Public Health Reports, 71:* 1027–1030, 1956.

Johnson, A. M.: Collaborative psychotherapy: team setting. In Marcel Heiman: *Psychoanalysis and Social Work.* New York, Intl Univs Pr, 1953.

MacGregor, R., Ritchie, A. M., Serrano, A. C., Schuster, F. P., Goolishian, H. A., and McDanald, E. C.: *Multiple Impact Therapy.* New York, McGraw, 1964.

Peck, H. B.: An application of group therapy to the intake process. *Am J Orthopsychiatry, 23:* 338–349, 1953.

Serrano, A. C.: *Multiple Therapy.* Unpublished manuscript, 1973.

Whitaker, C. and Napier, A.: A conversation about co-therapy. In Farber, Mendelshon, and Napier: *The Book of Family Therapy.* Science House, 480–506, 1972.

Whitaker, C. A., Warkentin, J., and Johnson, N. L.: A philosophical basis for brief psychotherapy. *Psychiatr Q, 23:* 439–443, 1949.

Zuk, G. H.: *Family Therapy: A Triadic-based Approach.* New York, Behavioral Publications, 43–82, 1971.

CHAPTER 9

GROUP MARITAL THERAPY

John G. Cull and Richard E. Hardy

●●

MARITAL ROLES IN GROUP COUNSELING

RELATIONSHIPS NECESSARY FOR EFFECTIVE
GROUP INTERACTION

GROUND RULES FOR GROUP MARITAL
SESSIONS

TIME PERIODS AND TYPES OF SESSIONS

REFERENCES

●●

MARITAL ROLES IN GROUP COUNSELING

OFTEN IT IS DIFFICULT to discriminate between actual behavior and behavior which is related by a marriage partner. This period of counseling is difficult; the marriage counselor is interacting on a one-to-one basis or is occasionally seeing both marriage partners together. As a result of the defensiveness and the ego-protective nature of the individual client, quite often there is a great degree of uncertainty in the mind of the therapist as to the reality of the roles which are being reported to him, and, when it is evident that there is a reality base for some of the reports he receives from an antagonistic spouse, the question remains concerning the impact of this reported role, the substance of the role, and its prevalence. When a marriage starts deteriorating, it is quite natural for each partner to try to justify his position and to displace blame and responsibility for the deterioration of the marriage through recriminations and the imputing of negative roles to the other partner.

Group work is an ideal approach to be used in separating and understanding these diverse roles which are so basic in the marital interaction. As the therapist observes the individuals and their roles within the group, he can make a direct connection between the role an individual adopts in the group setting and the one he tends to play most often in the marital setting. In individual counseling, the client may appear somewhat passive, withdrawn and taciturn, and relate his reaction to others and his reaction to events in a philosophical manner. However, in group interactions, it is quite possible for him to change drastically and become the aggressor rather than the passive receptor in a relationship. The following types of behavior are deleterious to a marriage and may be observed in the marriage relationship. We will discuss them as they fall along a continuum from highly aggressive behavior through the acceptance seeker, the sympathy seeker, the confessor, the externalizer, the isolate, the dominator, and the antagonist. Many of these roles will not be exhibited in individual counseling with the marriage partner; however, the group therapist will see them emerge as the group begins to interact.

The Aggressive Individual

As mentioned above, an individual may appear somewhat passive in his relationship to others, and his reaction to events makes him appear as passive receptor in a relationship. However, when observed in a group setting, it may become obvious that a drastic change has occurred and, in reality, he is a highly aggressive individual. As an aggressor, he may work many ways to exert his will. He may be oblivious or unconcerned about the feelings of others. He may override their concerns by deflating them and attempting to relegate them to lower status, either expressing disapproval of or ignoring their feelings, their value system, or the acts in which they engage which are counter to his basic goals. He will appear to be highly goal-oriented regardless of the cost in achieving that goal, and he will work toward the goal regardless of the hurt feelings and the damage to his interpersonal relationships. He works toward the goal which he perceives as the one bringing him most recognition. Under this set of circumstances, this individual will be most manipulative in that he will show the highest degree of Machiavellianism in the group. He will be somewhat jealous of individuals who gain more recognition than he, and he will be sympathetic toward the individual whom he outshines most readily. Yet this individual may see himself as a somewhat passive person and have little or no understanding of the obvious sources of marital discord.

The Acceptance Seeker

Related to the individual who has a high degree of need to accomplish the goals he perceives as important and who accomplishes them through aggressive-type behavior is the individual whose concern is not the accomplishment of the goals, but whose goal is to receive acceptance by the group or one who feels the need for recognition within the group. This is an individual who is quite insecure and tends to need almost continual positive reinforcement as to his self-adequacy and his value to the group or to the marriage partner. This type of individual demonstrates his needs in the group in many ways. Generally, he will not be as oriented toward the goal, which is perceived by the group as the group goal, as well as the aggressive-type individual. But he will work toward the goal if he feels it will bring a great deal of recognition. Much of his overt behavior upon examination will be seen to be self-serving and self-gratifying behavior rather than goal-oriented behavior. It has been our experience, in group work with marriage partners, that this type of individual has many more needs than the aggressive-type individual. If the individual, who is seeking the recognition to the exclusion of everything else, has a spouse who attempts to meet these needs, quite often the needs are so great the spouse loses the impact she once had to fulfill his needs; therefore, he looks elsewhere for the recognition which is so essential to his personality integration. He responds to her as being unconcerned about him, as not really understanding his motivations, and may give the impression that the spouse is somewhat self-centered and uncooperative in the marriage pact. In the group situation, the individual demonstrates his need for recognition by behavior and mannerisms both verbal and non-verbal which call attention to himself. He quite often will boast; he will feel the need to relate personal experiences; he will relate his accomplishments and achievements; perhaps he may relate them in a thinly veiled manner under the guise of using them as an example to make a point in some other area; however, he feels compelled to bring forth his accomplishments, his values, his attributes to the group and to hold them out for group approval. His most painful moments in the group will be when he perceives he has been devalued by other members in the group and placed in an inferior position or when he feels he is demonstrating behavior which is characterized by the group as inadequate.

The Sympathy Seeker

On a continuum down from the aggressive-type individual to the individual who is seeking recognition from the group, the next type of personality may be characterized as the sympathy seeker. This individual attempts to elicit responses of sympathy from the group, thereby obviating any pressures for him to achieve either within the group or without the group. As he depreciates himself and relegates himself to a lower inferior position, he gets the sympathy of the group and at the same time is absolved of responsibility within the group. This provides him a haven of irresponsibility. He is able to go his own way; he can follow the group or he can elect to remain aloof from the group, all with the approval of the group as a result of his being in a position to receive sympathy from the group. As the group becomes more demanding and insistent on his con-tributing, he will reinforce his protestations of inferiority or illness, of devaluation, or of a generalized inadequacy. He will attempt to reinforce the group's feelings of sympathy for him in order to free himself from entanglements of the group. If he is unsuccessful in his attempts to get sympathy from the group, he will attempt to split the group into smaller units and will seek statements of sympathy from the smaller subgroups. The value of the group interaction is to denote how an individual, who is a sympathy seeker in the group setting but who, in the marriage relationship and during individual counseling, may come through as a relatively independent sort of person who expresses feelings of adequacy and concern for the marriage relationship, will change when his behavior is observed and the pressures of the group are exerted.

The Confessor

The next type of behavior which is brought out in a group is the confessing behavior. This is behavior that is characterized by rather superficial confessing. As the individual sees that the demands to reveal himself are getting greater and as he sees that his responsibility will have to be fulfilled if he is to maintain membership in the group, quite often he starts confessing in a very superficial manner to the group. Generally, these confessions are characterized by large quantity with very low quality. He feels that the more he confesses, the more he absolves himself of responsibility for honest group interaction. He confesses to his feelings, which are somewhat insignificant, in a very sober, concerned fashion. He professes to have immediate insight as a result of the group sessions. When an individual starts to criticize him, this confessing-type individual immediately stifles the criticism or stifles the comments by agreeing with the critic and by going even further in confessing on and on *ad nauseum* these feelings or attributes and related feelings and attributes.

In a marriage, confessing-type behavior is a very effective defense. It is quite frustrating when a marriage partner tries to communicate and is thwarted by the other marriage partner's superficial self-confessing behavior. Communication is effectively blocked when one marriage partner evades a confrontation with the other marriage partner by this superficial type of confessing behavior. When this type of behavior is exhibited, it is quite difficult to get to the core of the problem in individual counseling since the confessor is verbalizing a great deal of concern, flexibility, and willingness to cooperate when, in fact, his behavior is aimed more at stifling communication and blocking effective understanding within the marriage relationshp. By adopting this defensive behavior, he is not required to engage in a confrontation with the other marriage partner. He is able to maintain interaction on a relatively superficial level.

The Eternalizer

Another type of behavior which is exhibited in groups can be characterized by the term "externalization." The externalizer is an individual who becomes uncomfortable in the interaction and the "give and take" which is occurring in the group or which occurs in close interpersonal relationships; he tends to focus on problems that are external to the group or external to the relationship. As the group starts to focus on the individual or gets too close to the individual, he starts externalizing in order to shift the brunt of an attack or of an inquisition from him on to some external object. Quite often this can be a very effective maneuver; however, again, it is one which is highly frustrating to an individual who is seriously trying to resolve conflicts. An effective externalizer is able to communicate his values, his impressions, his attitudes and beliefs very effectively without referring to himself. He does this through interjecting or projecting his attitudes into the attitudes of groups external to the interaction he is currently engaged in. Consequently, he is able to communicate a point of view which he holds without allowing others to adequately communicate their point of view.

The Isolate

The next type of behavior which is observed in the group setting and has a direct referent back to marital interactions is the isolate. This is the individual who decides to insulate himself from the interaction of the group. He very definitely elects not to interact with the group and decides to disallow the group to interact now with him. He quite often will make a very studied effort to inform the group of his nonchalance, of his decision to be noninvolved. He does this quite often by engaging in stratagems which are distracting to the group but which give no indication of his interest or willingness to contribute to the group. He may attract the attention of one or two other members of the group and start to play with them. He may become animated in doodling. He may develop little games which he plays with himself such as folding paper, making airplanes, drawing pictures of the room. When confronted, his general response is, "I'm paying attention," "I'm listening," "I'm participating," "I just engage in these little activities to heighten my sensitivity to what's going on." This individual generally will not allow himself to be drawn into the interaction within the group. He will stay outside the mainstream of activity and will attempt to communicate his intentions to stay outside the mainstream of activity through nonverbal behavior. His verbal behavior will be one of conciliation and concern.

The Dominator

The next type of behavior, on the continuum from highly goal-oriented to highly negativistic, will be the individual who tries to dominate one or more individuals in the group or tries to dominate the entire group. His drives toward domination are an effort to convince others of his authority and of his superiority. His interests are not as goal-oriented as the aggressive-type individual who sacrifices others' feelings and his own interpersonal relationship with others in an effort to accomplish a group goal; however, the dominating-type individual is concerned with exerting influence over others, not for the goal which can be achieved, but just for the sake of dominance. If there is a highly aggressive individual in the group and a dominating individual in the group, the more maladaptive type of behavior will be exhibited by the dominating individual, for he will find the need to express his adequacy by wooing group members away from the goal-oriented, aggressive-type individual whose drives are to move the group toward a goal. The dominator will achieve his purpose if he subverts the actions or intents of the aggressive individual. The dominating individual is concerned with achieving a status of respect. He may do this through many types of behavior, such as being punitive and using the threat of punitive behavior to cower a weaker member. He may use flattery to woo a member. He may use the power of suggestion and persuasion, or he may just attempt to verbally and socially overpower the other individuals to force them into submission. In a marriage relationship, this type individual most often has to have a wife who is somewhat passive and one who does not have a high level of need for individuality and expressions of self-adequacy through the approval of their spouse.

The Antagonist

The next and last type of behavior to be discussed is the antagonist. This is the individual who strives for self-adequacy and recognition through the negativistic behavior and values he adopts. He is somewhat arbitrary and capricious in his value judgments. The underlying constant of his judgments is the contrariness of his position. He seems to be at odds with the mainstream of opinion, values, or actions within the group interaction. His negativism can be quite harsh and sharp. He apparently is unconcerned about the feelings of others in the group. The most important thing to him is to exhibit his individuality by disagreeing with the group consensus. He is stubbornly resistant to coercion or persuasion. He will go so far as to disrupt the flow of the work of the group by attempting to change directions, to change the topic of concern, to alter the goal which the group is working toward, or to try to redefine the ground rules which were established in the group. This antagonist takes a negative view of life and is antagonistic to almost all of the members in the group. He is argumentative and can be quite bombastic when thwarted.

Individual and Group Approaches

There is an exercise in group behavior which requires working toward the solution of a problem concerned with being marooned on the moon. The problem requires individuals to react by rank, ordering a number of various types of equipment which they would choose to have with them if they were so marooned. The exercise, which has been checked by space experts at the National Space and Aeronautics Administration, is first completed by individuals and later by a group of six to eight persons working together. The usual result of the exercise is that group behavior is demonstrated, over and over again, to be more effective in getting at correct solutions to problems than is individual effort alone. In some few cases, the individual's decision may be more effective than that of the group, but, in most cases, the group decision is more nearly correct than the individual one.

The purpose of the exercise is to demonstrate the effectiveness of group interaction in problem solving. Just as the exercise does demonstrate the effectiveness of increased interaction among individuals in problem solving, so does group marital counseling achieve much more in many cases than does the basic interaction between the client and therapist. While much can be accomplished by individual sessions with the client, it is our feeling that supplemental group sessions can bring about enormous strides in understanding and adjustment.

In marital counseling, it is essential to see the clients in an individual one-to-one situation. It is equally important to see spouses together; however, we feel that it is of utmost importance for effective marriage counseling to supplement individual counseling with group techniques, for it is through group techniques that much of the behavior, which can remain enigmatic in individual counseling, is delineated and exemplified by pressures and interactions of the group. Much of the behavior which has constituted irritant factors of the marriage pact are elicited in the group situation. This type of behavior is on the surface in the group. It can be observed by the therapist and in individual sessions which follow can be related to the individual and interpreted for him to review and evaluate and react to. Without benefit of the group, marital counseling is much slower and a much longer process. Many times, marriage will continue to deteriorate at a faster rate than the therapist is able to diagnose and treat the irritants which are precipitating the deterioration.

Selection of Group Participants

In group marital counseling, one generally has a decision to make concerning whether he wants to have in his group only husbands, only wives, or a mixed group. He also needs to make a decision whether husbands and wives will be in the same group. When husband and wife are in the same group, other members of the group can help them explore in considerable detail their problem areas. When husbands or wives are in groups made up of exclusively all males or all females, the group leader will experience some difficulty in keeping the session from turning into a type of complaint session about the opposite sex. When husbands and wives are in groups separate from one another, group members have been shown to be very eager to help the individual explore his marital situation and understand it more fully. The best combination seems to be one in which both husband and wife are in the same group or husband or wife are in mixed groups of males and females. Heterogeneity has a great affect upon effectiveness in group interaction and problem solving. Diversity brings with it a certain breadth of experience and increases the strength of the group to solve both individual problems and group problems. Persons from all walks of life can be mixed in a heterogeneous marital group-counseling situation. This same opinion would extend to persons of various ages and socioeconomic backgrounds.

RELATIONSHIPS NECESSARY FOR EFFECTIVE GROUP INTERACTION

Some of the necessary ingredients for effective group problem exploration include acceptance of others, awareness, self-acceptance of individuals in the group, and problem-centering approaches to behavior. When these conditions exist, a high "trust" level has been achieved. People are free to be themselves when a level of trust has been established in the group. When the "trust" level has not been established or is low, group members tend to be manipulative, to hold back information about themselves, and to be defensive. When individuals within the group trust one another, defensiveness is reduced, information flow is multiplied, and the strategies of manipulation are dissipated.

The group leader must create in members a feeling of freedom. They can be most valuable as group members to others in groups and themselves when they are free and able to be themselves.

Modeling Behavior

It is the responsibility of the group leader to model the types of behavior which he would like to see exhibited by the various members of the group. The group facilitator or leader should not be overbearing or dominating as a leader, but should move the group toward understanding of problems through various behaviors which he not only demonstrates but models. The group leader should be an individual who is friendly, warm, and accepting. He should be a person who works with others and does not practice techniques upon them. The word "with" suggests that the procedure taking place is a relationship and not a technique-oriented process. The atmosphere within the group should be productive of or conducive to good mental and social-psychological health. The goal of all group work is that of the obtainment of good mental health.

Every member of the group should be accorded enough consideration and respect by the group so that he has, at least, a modicum of self-esteem. The individual must be willing and able to accept himself within a group setting. He must feel that he has the respect of others and that he is a person of worth. The group environment should facilitate the development and maintenance of self-esteem.

Members of the group should show considerable acceptance of others and their attitudes, regardless of whether or not group members agree with the attitudes or ideas which are being expressed. In other words, group members do not have to agree with the ideas in order to accept them as legitimate personal feelings of the individual expressing them. At times, the needs of individuals in the group for self-esteem may interfere with their accepting and respecting others. It has been shown many times that we may want to feel superior to others and we do this by bolstering ourselves. When this is the case, often the person involved does not have enough respect for himself; therefore, he cannot respect others. Listening to another is the simplest and one of the most basic ways through which we can show respect for him.

Group members need to show understanding of others' feelings and the group leader should demonstrate that he understands how others feel and wishes to get to know them better. If the group leader uses psychological terminology glibly, he may "turn off" the group. He should not attempt to demonstrate understanding through such use of professional jargon, but he should demonstrate that he has what has been called accurate empathy in reference to the individual. He can put himself in the other's place and understand feelings as the other person experiences them.

All members of the group must demonstrate some degree of confidence in the other persons in the group. There must be recognition of the rights and privileges and freedoms to action of others. The group must be characterized by sincerity, integrity, openness, and honesty if it is to achieve its goals. These characteristics help eliminate the threat and help to create an environment in which the individual can develop to his fullest potential by exploring all aspects of his particular marital problem. The group leader should give his attention, respect, understanding, and interest to those within the group who are attempting to work toward a solution of their problems and help others to do likewise.

Artificiality must be avoided on the part of the group leader at all costs. There is no real alternative to genuineness in the group counseling process.

The group leader must demonstrate the types of behavior which participants in the group need to exhibit if problem solving is to take place. There must be a certain amount of risk-taking; in other words, individuals in the group must go beyond what is known to be factual in order to explore their behavior. Persons must be willing to do more than play it safe. If, for instance, within a session an individual becomes angry or anxious, these behaviors can make him appear foolish; but these may be necessary behaviors and necessary risks to take in order for him to achieve success in problem solving. There must be substantial support for others as members attempt to reach goals that are important. Persons can say in various ways that they may not be sure what an individual is aiming toward or proposing, but they support the efforts being made to get something moving or to make others understand a particular problem.

There should be a demonstration that persons are free and able to be open about their feelings and thoughts, and there should be a problem-centering, or focusing on problems faced by a group, rather than focus on control or method. Problem-centering is based upon the assumption that the group can accomplish much more when individuals in groups learn how to solve problems than when the leader has to employ certain technique patterns in order to achieve goals. Group members should clearly recognize the feelings of others and how one's feelings are interinfluencing the behavior of others.

Another characteristic which is most important in achieving the level of problem-solving ability necessary for success is that of the individual feeling that he can accept his own emotions without denying them or giving rationalizations or apologies. Such acceptance can be evidenced by such statements, "I am disgusted or bored with myself because I feel ineffective."

Problems Which May Surface During Group Marital Counseling

There is no end to the types of human situations which may come to light during marital counseling. Group marital counseling, just as individual counseling and other group counseling, covers the whole realm of human life and experience. Of course, there are sex problems which include frigidity, sterility, impotence and others. There are the problems of children, of incongruencies in expectations, of differences in opinion concerning careers, of extramarital relationships, of changing life styles in a rapidly moving society, and of parents and in-laws and their influence in the marriage. There are identification problems, problems of personal values, the different meanings of love, and substitutes for it, which are meaningful to some people and not meaningful to others, the expression and management of feelings, the handling of various financial crises, and many others. The counselor concerned with group marital counseling must be a mature individual who is able to facilitate human learning through the demonstration of the behaviors described earlier. He must know group interactions well and thoroughly understand human behavior.

GROUND RULES FOR GROUP MARITAL SESSIONS

Human interaction includes two major properties: (1) content and (2) process. Content has to do with the subject matter with which the group is concerned. Process has to do with the actual procedure of what is happening between and to group members while the group is working. The group leader must be sensitive to the group process in order to help the group in diagnosing special problems so that these can be dealt with soon and effectively.

One of the important concepts in group interaction is that everyone who is in the group belongs there because he simply is there. (Gendlin, 1968) has indicated that this concept is one of the most important ones in effecting successful group behavior. If an individual gets angry with another person, this behavior does not change his belonging in the group. If a person reads himself out of a group, it does not change his belonging in it. If he gives up on himself, the group does not give up on him.

Each person determines what is true for him by what is in him according to Gendlin. Whatever he feels makes sense in himself and whatever way he wishes to live inside himself is determined by what is in him as an individual. Most people live mostly inside themselves. No one knows more about how a person really is than the person himself. The group leader should remember that he should force no one to be more honest than he wants to be just at the moment he is speaking. We should listen for the person who is inside the individual who is living and feeling. This person may not be totally exposed to us at any given time although he may wish to be exposed.

The group leader is always responsible for protecting the belongingness of every member to the group and also his right to be heard. He is also responsible for the confidential aspect of the group disclosures, which means that no one will repeat anything which has been said outside of the group unless it concerns only himself.

Everyone should participate in the group. One indication of involvement is verbal participation. The group leader should look for differences in terms of who are the high and low participators. What are the shifts in participation. How are the persons who are not participating being treated by the others? What subgroups are there? Who keeps the group moving? Which of the groups are high in terms of influence? Are there autocrats and peacemakers? Are there members getting attention by their apparent lack of involvement in the group? Who attempts to include everyone in group discussion decision making? In other words, what are the styles of influence? Is that group drifting from topic to topic? Is this a defensive type of behavior? Do they attempt to become overly organized at the expense of the losing effectiveness in problem solving? Are there persons outside of the group?

Is the group avoiding certain topics and setting certain norms for behavior? Is religion or sex avoided, for instance, as a topic? Are the group members being overly nice to each other? Are they agreeing too soon? In short, are they avoiding facing individual and group problems?

One of the helpful techniques which can be used in group marital counseling is that of spontaneous role playing. This can be done by husband and wife actually sitting in the center of the group and playing out a particular problematic situation. The group members can then react to various aspects of the role playing and make suggestions in order that the individuals may develop fuller understanding of the problem area. It may also be useful to have a surrogate wife or husband role play with an actual husband or wife.

Role reversal is another technique in which individuals reverse their roles and then role-play actual situations. This technique can be most interesting in that the husband plays the wife's part and wife plays the husband's part. It is sometimes easy to bring about understanding through the use of this technique. Persons can relive past events or project future occurrences through role playing.

Another technique which is useful is that of repeating the client's key words or statements. This is particularly useful in terms of what has been called free association, in other words, that process of using clues or cues to help the client give meaningful information about himself and his problems.

The group leader should keep in mind that persons who have many psychosomatic complaints may be disguising personal problems and conflicts. He should also remember that the individual group member who offers any complaints about his spouse may be covering his own personal anxieties and inadequacies.

TIME PERIODS AND TYPES OF SESSIONS

The purpose of this chapter has been to describe group marital counseling. Generally, sessions may last for three to four hours and may be ongoing, meeting eight to ten or more times. This varies from the individual counseling sessions which usually last from fifty to sixty minutes.

Much of the material given in this chapter concerns the facilitating of groups rather than the actual leading of them as a group therapist. It is felt by the authors that selected encounter group concepts can be of substantial benefit in various types of marital counseling.

Of course, it may be that group members will wish to engage in a type of marathon encounter in which they may continue their group activities for twenty to twenty-four hours. These sessions can later be followed by shorter two-to-three-hour sessions follow-up groups for those who are interested. Group leaders should not become discouraged if some of their group members do not choose to return to later group meetings. People vary enormously in their abilities to withstand various types of stress, and many people feel a good deal of insecurity and stress during group counseling work, even though substantial efforts have been made to establish an atmosphere of warmth and trust. Some people are able to gain a great deal in a short period of time and, for these persons, individual counseling may be more in accordance with their needs than group experiences.

The group counselor, leader, or facilitator—whichever name is chosen—must keep in mind that the purpose of the session is whatever goal the group decides upon. At times a group session may provide real service in terms of being informational in nature. One of the basic problems related to problems in marriage is the preparation for simply living with another person.

At times, the counselor will find it necessary to assume the role of information giver and tutor in individual sessions, and in group sessions members find it necessary to be informational in order to achieve basic goals which have been established. Group members can greatly help individuals in the group by exploring the needs of each person. In many cases unmet needs exist due to the fact that these needs are not understood by the spouse and often the person himself.

REFERENCES

Gendlin, E. T., and Beebe, J.: Experiential groups: Instructions for groups. In G. M. Gazda (Ed.): *Innovations to Group Psychotherapy*. Springfield, Thomas, 1968, pp. 190–206.

CHAPTER 10

"I DON'T LIKE MYSELF"

E. RAY JERKINS

●●

FINANCES AND INITIATIVE

SEX AND MOTIVATION OR AGGRESSIVENESS

INITIATIVE AND HOW TO SAY "NO"

INITIATIVE AND CHILD-DISCIPLINE

SUMMARY

●●

So MANY TIMES when we deal with marital problems we spend our time trying to decide how the spouse feels about his mate. I believe that time should be spent in determining how much the person thinks of himself. Generally this particular trait will show itself in many important areas such as sex, handling of finances, discipline of children, holding a job and being promoted, and in the making and holding of friends.

There are those who have what I usually like to speak of as a "lack of initiative." They have a hard time saying "no," are easily led, tend to emphasize the importance of others and belittle themselves, rarely really express their opinions, and tend to be thought of as lazy. How do you deal with the person who feels that he is not as good as others, who feels that he is not included in activities because he isn't good enough, who does not take up for himself, and who many times will pretend illness or tiredness to avoid a difference of opinions? This person will many times remind you of the little orphan who once described his plight by saying, "Shucks, I ain't nobody's nothin."

Now, what are the problems that this attitude will create in the family? You will find it in all phases of the marriage. I will briefly note these—finances, sex, saying "No," and child-discipline—and then will come back for a more complete discussion. In interviewing conjointly, you will many times find this trait exhibited when one completely overrules and always corrects the other and the spouse allows himself to be corrected and overruled. Is this merely a courtesy gesture or is it a lack of initiative?

When complaints are listed, you will find statements like: "I have to make all of the decisions;" I have to be husband and wife;" "he can't ever make up his mind." "She resents her friends because they take advantage of her;" "She (he) drinks constantly;" "She is a poor housekeeper." The list can go on and on, but these will help you see that one area that needs direction is that of self-motivation, or initiative, or even aggressiveness.

FINANCES AND INITIATIVE

There is probably no area where self-control or personal initiative is more necessary than in the area of finances. Easy credit, pressure advertising, peer group standing and poor planning keep many people in a poor financial condition. I usually begin by suggesting a plan to help them take a stand on their convictions. I ask both to agree not to spend fifty dollars for any one thing, excluding food, without the consent of the spouse.

For example, suppose the husband finds a fishing outfit or accessory, that he feels he desperately needs, that costs $54.95. Under this plan, he cannot make the purchase until he talks it over with his wife and they both agree. Or, suppose the wife finds an appliance that she wants to buy for $52.50. She cannot make the purchase until she discusses it with her husband. Their spending is taken out of the "impulsive" area and gets both the husband and the wife in on the dispersal of their funds.

Suppose that one spouse asks the other about the proposed purchase and there is complete disagreement. They cannot argue about it for hours, but only thirty minutes.[1] If no agreement is reached, the subject is dropped for three weeks; many times this three-week period is enough to cool things down and the interest in making the purchase will be diminished. After three weeks the subject can be discussed again; if no agreement is reached, it is dropped for one more week and then brought up again.

When I have a couple genuinely trying to make a go of their marriage, I find that compromises will be worked out in this month's time. If no agreement is reached, the purchase is not made. But I do point out that both of them will want to make purchases over fifty dollars at times, and by working together—not against each other—they will be able to use their money more wisely.

Many problems are not caused by large financial purchases, but, as one client stated, "We are just nickeled and dimed to death." This is often the case when people get satisfaction from spending. With them, we begin by asking, "Which gives greater satisfaction, this small article that says, "buy me," or being able to say, "I can say 'No'?" Ask the question, "Do I really need this?" If you need additional time to make up your mind about the purchase, put it off for thirty minutes. Walk around in the store or go on down the mall and then decide if you should buy this "small," one- or two-dollar item.

We are speaking here of the person who has money, and it is just "burning a hole in his pocket." We are trying to give him the self-motivation to say "NO." These little built-in ideas

---

[1] Very early in counseling I give the rules for arguing; which are as follows: 1) A couple is permitted to argue for thirty minutes once a day on one subject only. 2) Nothing more than two weeks old can be introduced. 3) There can be no arguing until one hour after arising and it must stop two hours before bedtime. 4) There can be no violence or profanity. 5) "Hollering" is permitted so long as the voice cannot be heard outside your living quarters. 6) Arguments must be private, not before the children and not at meals.

are merely ways to provide time to get him away from the point of "temptation" and to get his mind focused on something else. It gives him time to really think through the reason why he is buying.

SEX AND MOTIVATION OR AGGRESSIVENESS

It is difficult to use pronouns here for fear that someone might think all sex problems are with the female and not the male, or vice versa. From my experience, it seems as though it is as much with one as the other. However, lack of initiative or self-confidence is often evident and causes problems. Sex ought to be spontaneous on the part of both. Neither should necessarily sit back and wait for the other spouse to always make the first move. If one lacks self-confidence to "perform" or if there is a lack of aggressiveness because of continued rejection, this area needs investigation.

Sex is definitely a matter of moods and of attitude for both male and female. Not often do you find a physiological problem that prevents satisfying sexual relationships, and, if so, it can usually be remedied through medical assistance. How can we deal with the problem of the spouse who would like to take the aggressive role but who lacks self-confidence?

I recommend that he prepare himself by visualizing the approaching incident as vividly as possible. To do this, it is best to concentrate on it intensely for at least thirty minutes a day. While intensely imagining what is going to happen the way he wants it to happen, he actually practices or goes thru the motions of his movements toward his spouse. He practices out loud the words he is going to use. At this point he is bringing his entire mind to concentrate on the action he is going to take. Later it will seem routine because he has already gone over it so thoroughly in his mind. He is building up confidence by seeing himself successfully complete the act, even if it is only in his mind. "As a man thinketh in his mind (heart) so is he." He is not just wishing himself successful; he is actually seeing himself successful and believing that he has done and can do it enjoyably.

Sometimes you, the counselor, must start with something

other than the giving of an exercise; you must ascertain the reason for the lack of confidence. Did it come from the spouse and their home life, from school activities, or from the job? Your encouragement can be most beneficial. For instance, one lady stated that she would like to make advances to her husband but felt that "good girls" didn't do that. Investigation revealed that her idea had been formed many years earlier by her parents and by a teacher. She realized during counseling that hers was not a proper attitude. To overcome the attitude of the past and help her to a better relationship with her husband, I supported her with positive sessions and assignments of mental exercises. All of them were to show her that she had the ability and to teach her that her new image and role were not wrong.

INITIATIVE AND HOW TO SAY "NO"

So many times you get involved in outside activities, and you want to kick yourself because you could not or did not say "no." You didn't say "no" because you were afraid to hurt anyone's feelings or you didn't know how to refuse graciously. These outside involvements do cause problems, especially when the spouse feels that families and friends are taking advantage of you. How do you say "no" without hurting someone's feelings or without using improper terms? You begin by practicing the refusal, what you say and how to say it. Suppose you are called on the phone and asked to do something, your reply is, "I certainly do appreciate your thinking of me and wanting me to do this, but may I call you back in a few minutes? I need to check on a couple of things first." You have made your first refusal, you have thanked the caller for thinking of you and wanting you to do the job. I suggest that you wait thirty minutes before you make the decision or return the call. During this time you can plan what you are going to say. Go to the mirror, practice how you are going to phrase your answer, and go over it several times, this will work. Now when you are ready to return the call, again express your appreciation for interest and thoughtfulness BUT . . . . Then you regretfully decline but you DO NOT HAVE TO EXPLAIN WHY!

But if the request is made not on the phone but face to face, how do you handle it? Again, your first statement is, "I certainly do appreciate it, but may I check on a couple of things first, so I can know what my schedule is?" You have not immediately refused, but have given yourself time to formulate the proper words for your declination.

Let me discuss more fully the idea that I have just presented about practicing what to say; it will work in many situations. I frequently ask my clients if they ever talk out loud to themselves. If they do not, I encourage them to begin; in this way, they can plan ahead how they are going to say whatever is on their minds.

Practicing can take place in front of the mirror but should always be done in private. (An old wives' tale that talking to oneself is a mark of insanity, is not true.) Every speaker, teacher, salesman, and others dependent on the spoken word to influence the listener, diligently practices what and HOW he is going to speak. In this way, he becomes familiar with the words, their sounds, their inflections, and their possible impact. As he becomes familiar with the phrases, he becomes more comfortable. The more one practices, the better the words will come, even though he may become frightened or upset. In a sense, he is programming his mind with certain words and phrases that will come forth almost automatically when he is ready for them.

This practicing is important in every field—love-making, child-discipline, social involvements, finances, job relationships, and, especially relations with in-laws.

INITIATIVE AND CHILD-DISCIPLINE

One who lacks the self-confidence and initiative will experience difficulty when it comes to training children. Those who are parents know the patience that is demanded to properly direct and rear children. There are times when it is much easier to be passive and let them do whatever they desire. For this reason, we have lived in the age of permissiveness. When one of the parents is "stern" in discipline and the other lacks the initiative and aggressiveness to direct, there are going to be problems. Such problems will be described in statements like, "The discipline is never the same. The child is punished today for something; he did the same thing yesterday and there was no punishment." "He (she) does not make the children mind." "Our children can get away with murder."

What are some practical suggestions for solving the problem of child-discipline? Here are a few:

1. Both parents should always agree in front of the children on disciplinary matters. If there is a disagreement let it be in private. Thinking parents will anticipate areas in which they might be divided. For instance, a difference about the time children should come in can be compromised by splitting the difference of the time; i.e. midnight could be the compromised time between eleven P.M. and one A.M. You know the child is going out, and so in anticipation, decide on the curfew time. This anticipation has to be a forced action on the part of the one with low inititiative and will have to be suggested by the other parent.

2. Recognize that the "job" of child-rearing is real and that it needs your attention. Make a list of the areas in which you, as a parent, must take an active part. These would probably be clothes, manners, educational matters, dating habits, visitation privileges, study habits, religion, finances, sex education, housekeeping, etc. Having made the list, ask yourself frankly how much you have done and what you could do in each area. Making of lists is important. On none of the listed items do you "take over," but you do become aware of some of your responsibilities. The results of making the list are that, even though your initiative is low, you have made a list, thought out the areas, considered your responsibilities. YOU HAVE DONE SOMETHING!

3. When you are aware that child-discipline is a problem area, seek out a family whose child-rearing you admire. Begin to observe their actions, decisions, and interfamily relationships, and, if necessary, ask them how they would handle a particular problem. You can follow the example of their relationship with their children.

SUMMARY

To deal with lack of initiative as a marital problem, we have to assist our client to gain more self-confidence. It can come through assignment of books that deal with the subject.

We must suggest that the spouse be more complimentary and less critical so that the ego will be supported and boosted. The spouse must be willing to be more positive in statements about himself and his mate. To be specific: I ask that each spouse make a list (including at least ten items) of his and his spouse's good qualities (strengths). This list furnishes me with a platform from which to work and permits me to view my clients' assets as seen by each and by his mate.

One of the great Biblical principles is, "Love thy neighbor as thyself." This means that we should love our associates as we love ourselves; but if we do not love ourselves, if we have low esteem for ourselves, we will not have a high regard for others. It is our concern as counselors, to assist clients to see their strengths, for they have already concentrated too long on their weaknesses.

THE FIRST INTERVIEW AND THE HISTORY

One of the most difficult problems in counseling is "getting the interview started properly so that your clients are at ease and willing to cooperate." For this reason, the first impression of these troubled people, desiring help, is most important.

It is necessary that your office be professional, yet warm, with emphasis on privacy. For instance, I do not use overhead lights, but lamps that give the room a soft atmosphere. Your office must be neat, uncluttered, business-like, conducive to encouraging your client to think, "Here is a man who means business and who is genuinely interested in me." For this reason, I do not recommend that your offices be in your home, which may leave the impression that this is a part-time job.

Your personal appearance is extremely important. Your mode of dress should be in very good taste, not out-of-date, yet not mod. Since you will be dealing with every taste, ideal, and standard, you must be cautious about dress. Even your facial expressions are important. You will have only a short period of time to set your clients at ease, gain their confidence, encourage their trust, and prepare them to honestly and completely confide in you; there may not be a second chance.

The establishment of a good relationship through your personality is important. You must realize that the situation is probably embarrassing to your clients and that it took a lot of courage for them to come. You, as counselor, can relieve the pressure by indicating that you are not "judge and jury." You should emphasize that you do not say that one has been a "bad boy or bad girl," and that it is not your work to sit in judgment on their set of values. In this way, your clients can remove their "masks" and can begin their story without fear of censure. Of course, you must always assure absolute confidentiality on your part. Even in the conjoint situations and later in the separate interviews, there must be no divulgence of confidential information to the other party.

Some things naturally arise in the first interview, and I often invite questions by saying. "Do you have any questions that you would like to ask me before we begin?" I usually get two or three standard ones, such as: "How long will this take?", "How much are your fees?", and "Are you recording this?"

"How long will this take?" Since absolute honesty is important, your best answer is, "I don't know." Success will depend upon the clients' cooperation and willingness to succeed. Remind them that they should not ask you to help them work out a solution in an hour or two hours to a problem that they have been getting into for two, five, ten, twenty, or twenty-five years. It is not easy to change their attitudes or ideas or to get them to respond to your suggestions that they do things differently from the way they have been doing them. If they want to know what success you have had, you must be on guard that you do not make any exaggerated claims of what you can do; this might cause them to have undue optimism or pessimism.

"How much are your fees?" As I am in private practice this is usually discussed and it should be discussed quite frankly. I use a session of fifty minutes which is referred to as "an hour." To avoid misunderstandings, be sure to state your rate as "so much per hour," not "so much per session."

"Are you recording this?" I do not make recordings, although some counselors do. If you record, it is best to so state and ask for the clients' permission at the very beginning; and, if you are recording, make it absolutely clear what you are doing.

In order to give your clients your absolute attention, you should take as few notes as possible. Much data will already be on an information sheet, a discussion of which follows, and you can easily make reference to this. You are now ready to get into the information sheet and your first session.

I begin the same with every client who comes to the office. This may sound absurd, but it is true and quite necessary. It is just standard operational procedure. I believe that, in order to solve the problem, we must first locate it. There is, therefore, no substitute for taking the history thoroughly at the first interview. For this reason, I have developed my own information sheet that will give me an almost complete view of my clients.

My information sheet begins with the date and the names of both husband and wife, especially her maiden name. This furnishes additional information, if the couple was reared locally, about background and social circles.

Next I ask the birthdates and birthplaces of both husband and wife. It is also necessary to know the areas in which they grew up. This information gives a definite idea as to the location of the in-laws and begins to help me see some additional problems, of which they are not aware, that might be involved. (Even though the Civil War has been over for a century, the battle is still going on between the two areas.)

The question of children immediately follows. It is important to know the *birthdates* and *names* of the children. In all future sessions, it is much better to refer to them by name, rather than as "your next-to-the-oldest child," etc. It is also important to know the birthplace of each child, because this gives the pattern of the couple's movements over the past several years and assists you in putting together the complete picture. The children's school grade and location should be added. At this point, children by a previous marriage will be so identified.

My next question as to the number of marriages is quite direct. If this is the second or third, it is always important to get the dates of the previous marriages. At a later session, I ask about the reason that previous marriages failed, grounds for divorce, the present location of previous spouses, and how often the children are visited.

It is important that the dates be quite specific because I now get to the one that gives additional insight: "When were you married?" Again I am specific about the exact date, not just the year. What does this date tell me? It tells several things. First, was she pregnant at the time of marriage, and, if so, how many months had passed? Of course, I do not necessarily point this out now, but at some point in the sessions it will come out. Secondly, were they dating each other during the previous marriage, and could this have caused it's failure? Third, did they wait long between marriages? Fourth, were they teenagers when married? If there is any difference in opinion as to the date of marriage, let them discuss it and settle on a time so you can have a reference point.

At this point, I have already been able to observe part of their relationship. As I begin taking the information, I never direct my questions to just one of them. I notice that one will take the lead in answering, one will begin to correct the other in a rather hostile way, or one will start and then the other completely take over the answers. This indicates fairly accurately what the home situation is. As the interview information sheet continues, I ask where and by whom they were married and if it was a religious or civil ceremony. This permits me to know to a degree their attitude toward marriage. Did they elope or was it just a quick drive over the state line? Was it a planned church wedding or was it at the office of a judge or justice of the peace? If it was religious, there was planning and you have some leverage of religion to use; it was possibly approved by the parents.

Now that the part on dates and background of their marital status is concluded, I ask about their housing. Do they own or rent their house? I am interested in knowing the size of the house and the number of bedrooms. This gives an idea as to the amount of privacy they might have. Many times remarks are made about the house that indicate unhappinesss with the living situation. I ask for approximate monthly payments for mortgage or rent so that I can see their handling of finances and if they are paying too much. One many times makes comments about the fact that they have been wanting to move, but . . . !

Next I inquire about occupations of both and how long they have been employed in their present work in order to find out about stability in holding a job. If there have been a succession of jobs, it is necessary to know the approximate dates of each and the reasons for leaving. This question permits me to have insight into their daily surroundings and into their ambitions. Are they with skilled or unskilled, professional or clerical people? What have been the marriage problems of other clients in similar fields?

Each time you ask for information, it must be done in an almost matter-of-fact way, indicating that the questions are merely routine and necessary. When I come to the one on income, I usually ask, "About how much do you make a year— not the penny amount but in round figures?" It is absolutely necessary to know this, because there is no way to competently counsel without it. It is necessary to know the income of *both* husband and wife.

At this point you will quite often receive some rather interesting answers. For instance, the husband may say, "I'd rather discuss this with you later." The wife may give a greater figure for her income than her husband. The husband might give an inflated figure and the wife tells him to be honest. One client might even refuse to give you the information. Refusal is very seldom, but it is an indication that you should look for a reason for this immediate mistrust or hostility.

There is another part of income that I had overlooked for a long time; but now I ask, "Do you have other sources of income?" This is important because it reveals payments being received for alimony or child support, trust fund income, or income from real property. Without this figure, you cannot properly assess the problem of finances, one of the areas in which you may be working.

The next field of information, important to counseling, is the education of the clients. I ask about their educational backgrounds and where they did their high school work. You can get a picture of their ability to comprehend any material you might assign. Their attitude about the education of their children is possibly revealed. Differences in educational backgrounds, such as a college degree for one and high school or less for the other, may be revealed. You then ask yourself why there is such a difference and if this could be a part of their problem.

Since religion is important, I ask the religion of each and that of their parents. My work, in the "Bible Belt," makes this information important, not to use as the lever in counseling, but to know if it may be a problem area. Did your clients break from their parental religion? Did one convert the other, and was the conversion sincere or for the sake of uniting the family in the one religion? One other dimension is: "When did you last attend?" The answer will give another side of the picture as to their concern about religion and what they are doing about their children. It will reveal if church attendance is creating a problem in that one thinks the spouse is a religious fanatic. Of course, you will need all of the help possible to assist the couple; if they happen to be religious people, you can appeal to their religious convictions.

Before I come to the final point of information, I ask about the family background. I need to know the ages of their parents, if they are still living, and if they are married, widowed or divorced? If divorced, when, and with whom were the children reared? I ask for the number of brothers and sisters and the place my clients have in their sibling structure, oldest, youngest, etc.

Because I am associated with a physician, I am greatly concerned with the medical background. Of both I ask, "Who is your family physician? What kind of surgery have you had? Have you ever been hospitalized?" What medication are you taking?" These questions are vitally important. I might emphasize that you do not comment on the physician or the medication or what the drugs do. The physician may be one who does not tell his patients the names of drugs. Knowing the drugs will help you at a later time to recognize any rather abrupt major changes which could be a reaction from the medication. I also ask, "Are you taking The Pill?" This gives the opening to learn the kind of birth control techniques employed and will reveal their attitude about sex that will assist your getting into that subject later.

Quite matter-of-factly you should ask, "How much do you drink?" There is a reason for asking the quantity rather than, "Do you drink?" Many times the answer will be, "That's part of the problem."

The history will include the name of the person who referred them to you. It will help you in your own records to know where your clients come from. If they are referred by a physician or attorney, it is certainly wise and appropriate to immediately write him a letter to express appreciation and to let him know that they did come.

SUMMARY

Only at this point do I feel that I am ready to start with the couple. Many times you will not have to ask the nature of the specific problem, for it will be apparent. You now have a complete view of practically every aspect of their family life and life style. You have information about their ages, family, marriage, occupation, education, finances, religion, medical background and the person responsible for their coming to you. There will be very little more factual information forthcoming.

TABLE 1

Date ————————— INTERVIEW INFORMATION FOR: ————

Birthdates: ——————————————————————————

H: —————————., Where? ————————————————————

W: —————————., Where? ————————————————————

Children: _____; Where _____

_____; Where _____

_____; Where _____

_____; Where _____

Number of marriages: H_____ W_____

When married: _____; Where? _____ By whom? _____

Housing: Own, rent?_____; Size_____ Monthly payment_____

Occupation: H_____ Length_____

W_____ Length_____

Annual Income: H_____; W_____; Other Sources_____

Education: H_____; W_____

Religion: H_____ Last attended? _____

H's parents_____

W_____ Last attended? _____

W's parents_____

FAMILY BACKGROUND: H's ages_____ M, D, W?_____

W's ages_____ M, D, W?_____

Brothers', sisters' ages _____

MEDICAL HISTORY: H:
(Family Physician)
(Surgery)
(Hospitalized)
(Deformities)
(Medication)
(Allergies)   W:
(Drugs, Alcohol)
(Abortions)
(The pill)

WHEN WAS THE LAST TIME YOU SAID, "I LOVE YOU?"

One of the most common problems I have deals with the expression (or lack of expression) of affection. At the close of my first session, I assign the following: List ten or more things that your spouse does that upsets you, and then list ten or more things that you do that upsets your spouse. The lists are not to be compared nor prepared together. When the area of affection is a problem, you will find statements like the following:

He treats me like his best buddy.

When I kiss him a lot he says, "Don't you ever get tired of that?"

He hugs and kisses me only when he wants to make love . . . not just because he likes hugging and kissing me.

I always have to initiate sex.

He is never at home.

He won't talk to me.

She has sexual hang-ups.

When I kiss her it is like kissing a stick.

He never comments about how I look unless it is a remark about something wrong with my clothes or hair.

She does not talk to me.

She does not want me to touch her.

He shows no interest around the house.

The list goes on and on and on.

There are many husbands and wives who are not expressive of their feelings. There is the adage, "Actions speak louder than words," but in marriage, not only the actions, but the words are necessary. Being demonstrative is largely a matter of communication. In the home you have two people who are supposed to be "in love;" yet they rarely have appreciative words or complimentary actions for each other. Even though the list above uses the term "he" several times, it does not mean that the problem is one that only men have. I have found that about as many men as women are restrained and repressed—unresponsive.

How can we overcome this particular problem? How will we teach the spouse to become more interested, or, at least, to express his affection? It must be thoroughly understood that expressiveness is a trait that has been learned, either consciously or unconsciously. As children grow up in the home, they are exposed to a teaching situation. They see their parents in the home interrelationships. If they never witness a demonstration of affection in the home, they are not "taught" that it is a proper way for husband and wife to act. It is good for children to see their parents embrace and show affection. It is also good for parents to display this affection toward their children. The general statement, used in defense of lack of expression of affection, is, "Well, I'm just not that type." It is believed that there is something biological or chemical that makes one cold, indifferent, and unconcerned. As counselors, we must assure our clients that the ability to express affection is a learned trait or characteristic.

There needs to be, and must be, physical and emotional warmth in the home if the couple is ever to reach the summit of marital happiness. Affection should begin in the kitchen in the morning, continue with kindness and consideration in the little things throughout the day, and come to the peak in the sexual relationship, which is the joining together of the two, both physically and emotionally. If there is no display of concern, interest, or affection at any time other than in the bedroom, there can be problems.

HOW TO BECOME MORE EXPRESSIVE OF YOUR FEELINGS

Since expressiveness is a trait that can be learned, we start with a self-teaching program. Let us suppose that it is almost impossible for you to say, "I love you." This is a little phrase that demands only a second and a-half of your time; but when I ask clients to learn to say it, they assure me that it will "choke them to death." However, just telling your clients to say "I love you" does not get it done.

I recommend that they start with talking out loud to themselves. This gets them used to hearing the words; saying it acquaints their minds with the words as well as the sound. As they continue to put this phrase in their vocabularies, they begin to visualize the scene when the phrase could and should be used. They may imagine the scene when the husband comes home or when the wife is greeted at the door. In their minds, they PLAY the scene and plan how they are going to use the term, "I love you."

Remembering special occasions, such as birthdays and anniversaries, is an expression of affection. Does he ever bring a small gift to his spouse just because he wants to share something with her? Love can be shown by preparing special meals or doing little things for him that he would like. And remember, there doesn't have to be a special occasion to do something nice. Mailing a card of affection keeps the romance and love alive. It says that he thinks of her and wants to share a little of his day, his time, and his thoughts with her. It doesn't have to be expensive; it is the thought that prompted him to do it that makes it of value.

I do caution my clients, however, by telling them of one incident when I had recommended that the husband occasionally take a small gift to his wife. One day he did stop at the store and bought a small bottle of perfume. When he walked in and handed it to her in the paper sack, he said, "Here. Mr. Jerkins said to buy you something!" Of course, you can imagine the result—disaster! It was done wrong.

Affection can be shown by the husband calling his wife to make a dinner date or to ask her to meet him for coffee or lunch somewhere. All he is doing is cultivating their relationship.

They replay the scene in their minds until it becomes almost second nature and they do not feel "up-tight" about saying the words. When they have practiced enough, maybe hours or days, depending on their desires and genuine interest, they will be surprised how easily the phrase comes and how relaxed they are in saying it.

Call all of this "romance" if you will, but it still has a place in a good marriage. We all like to have complimentary things said to us. But, if I ask the husband when he last complimented a meal, he usually says, "She knows I like it because I eat it. Don't I?" But, when he is invited out, doesn't he always have something complimentary to say to the hostess about the meal or the occasion? Simple manners should teach this. Why not do the same thing for his wife? How does he learn to be complimentary without sounding "gushy?" It is simple. He should plan what he would like to say and then practice the inflections and tone out loud. If he doesn't know what to say, he can listen to others as they compliment the hostess at a meal or to guests in his own home.

I suggest that my client decide what he would like to say about anything on any occasion. For example, some of the areas in which compliments would be in order are: clothing, hair, housekeeping, parties, planning, purchases, food and meal preparation, decorations, or any aspect of thoughtfulness, leadership, etc. When he has decided on the phrases (and it is best to make them short and simple), he should begin to make them a part of his "second nature" by practicing them and intensely imagining the situation in which they will be used. After proper practice and concentration, the phrases will almost "slip out" at the proper time. He will find them easy to say because he has already heard the words and knows what to say.

These simple directions have unlimited value. There are not many who really use their minds to the fullest. Whatever you put into your mind (through observation, for example) is what will come out. Much that you see can help you become "warmer." Movies, television programs, good books, plays, novels and friends are sources of object lessons on the expression of affection. If, for instance, you are reading a novel which has a part that deals with affection or a demonstration of concern for the spouse, read it aloud, over and over, to get the feel and sound of the words. You are teaching yourself and putting new ideas and thoughts into your mind. As you put them into your thinking, you begin to modify them to fit your needs and personality. As you practice them over and over and over, they become a real part of you. You are, in a sense, placing them in your mental computer.

It is a fact, just as it is that the sum of two and two is four, that you are not necessarily "phony" just because you are complimentary or show concern for another. You may rationalize about people whom you have considered to be phonies; but that doesn't mean that they were phony nor that you have to be false in your showing of affection. Remember the basis of your marriage should have been the giving of yourselves to each other; and in the marriage you are able to find satisfaction for each other. A part of us calls for affection or for someone to be interested in us. We must be able to see the good qualities in others and to express our appreciation, if in no other way, by saying, "Thank you."

When two people are in love, the loving pat or the affectionate touch speaks volumes. It might be wise to learn to touch; this does not mean the "laying on of hands" but a touch of love, a very gentle touch. It should be a slight brushing of the body, never rough, grabbing or bruising. When the hunter takes to the field with his dog and it performs well, he rewards it with patting its head, rubbing its body and even with a kind word; the dog then knows that it has done well. I doubt that it understands the words, but it knows the touch, the sound of the voice, and the friendly gestures.

Nearly every list of marital problems has sex near the top as one of the areas of difficulty. However, it is more likely that the lack of affection toward each other is the problem. Rarely do we find that biological difficulties or physical ailments are the major contributors to the break down in sex relationships. So, as the younger generation so aptly puts it, "What turned her (him) off?" Lack of affection is the reason that so many wives say, "All he wants from me is sex." This indictment of the husband results from his never showing any interest in her unless he wants sex and from showing no kindness or concern unless he "has one thing on his mind." Of course, this could be just as true of the wife.

When a couple complains that there is a sex problem, I look for what it is that "turns them off." If I get each to be more considerate, more concerned, just plain nicer, and if I can get them to think more of the other than of themselves, the "sex" problem will usually take care of itself. I realize that there are some areas of sex about which one spouse may have incorrect ideas; but when these ideas are corrected, it is still necessary to get into the area of being more demonstrative.

Doing things together, even just sitting and watching television or sitting and talking, is another way of showing affection. I often ask, "When was the last time you both sat down and just talked?" I don't mean a serious, deep discussion —just "talk" talk, like two friends getting together. Often the answers to that question indicate that it has been years— maybe never. But isn't this a way to show affection for a spouse? Doesn't this show that you enjoy his company and conversation?

One of the great needs we all have is the need for recognition. When you express yourself verbally, through gestures, by cards and gifts—by little things—you are saying, "You are somebody important to me and I am recognizing you for it by what I say and do." Both of these—saying and showing—are important. "How should one know that he is loved but by the way people act toward him: what they say, how they look, how they touch, in a word, what they DO? Attention, praise, spoken niceties, and physical contact have been demonstrations of love for years. Who cares if someone loves them if they never receive evidence through attention, contact or the spoken word?" [1]

---

[1] Madsen and Madsen, in David Knox, *Marriage Happiness: A Behavioral Approach to Counseling.* Champaign, Illinois, Research Press, 1971, p. 2.

CHAPTER 11

COUNSELING TECHNIQUES CASE STUDY DESCRIPTION

JOSEPH N. MERTZ

●●

CASE STUDY OF: MR. AND MRS. ALBERT AND CAROL E.

THE FIRST INTERVIEW

THE SECOND INTERVIEW: WITH MRS. E.

THE THIRD INTERVIEW: WITH MR. E.

THE NINETEENTH INTERVIEW

●●

WHEN I WAS approached to make a contribution to Marital Counseling: Case Study Descriptions, my first reaction was affirmative, since I have always felt that there was a real need for a practical, down-to-earth approach to the problem which many counselors encounter in marriage counseling. After I gave an affirmative response in terms of contributing material to this book, I became rather apprehensive when confronted with the task of attempting to present counseling sessions which would give the reader some insight and working knowledge about an actual case. The case which I have selected is not unique. However, it is a case that has many facets of disturbances and one that illustrates quite clearly how previous marital failures and disturbances can and do influence future marital ventures and the adjustments which both husband and wife are called upon to make if some measure of happiness and success is to be achieved.

CASE STUDY OF: MR. AND MRS. ALBERT AND CAROL E.

This is the case of a young couple known to me since April, 1971 and seen in regular weekly therapy sessions for a period of one year, after which therapy was gradually decreased until currently they are seen every three months on a maintenance level. Albert is 32, a graduate engineer, formerly married and divorced from his first wife in 1969, and the father of three children, all girls aged 9, 10, and 12, from that union. Carol is twenty-seven, is a Registered Nurse by profession, was formerly married for four years and divorced in 1969, and has no children by her former marriage. This couple was married in December 1970 after a courtship of a year and a half. Premarital sexual relations were entered into with some guilt response on behalf of Mrs. E.

Mr. and Mrs. E. were referred to my office by their minister. The problems were multiple and surfaced almost immediately after marriage. These were centered in what Mr. E. described as his wife's emotional state, "She's always upset. I'm afraid to say anything to her." He felt that she was scared of him and told her that she was foolish to feel like this. Mrs. E. on the other hand felt that she could not live up to her husband's expectations; she felt that he was continually making comparisons between his first wife and her. She admitted being fearful of speaking her mind to him and, as a result, communications broke down at all levels. An additional major complaint on behalf of Mrs. E. was her husband's lack of attention at an affectional and sexual level. These feelings were further highlighted by Mrs. E's desire to become pregnant and later learning that she was sterile. Adoption plans are now being worked through.

This abbreviated account of the presenting problems gives an indication of the multiplicity of problems confronting this couple. The therapy or counseling sessions cover a span of a year and a half. Initially sessions were on an individual basis, with joint sessions every four or five weeks. As insights were developed and the relationships stabilized, joint conferences were substituted for individual sessions.

THE FIRST INTERVIEW

When I first met this couple, I was impressed by their apparent genuine concern for one another and their marriage as a whole. I saw Mrs. E first and then her husband, these individual sessions being followed by a joint conference. This process, which for reasons of clarity I shall designate as a Diagnostic Session, normally takes an hour and a half. Usually I have only the barest essentials regarding a case and so must rely entirely on this initial contact to give me as concise and well-rounded a picture as possible of the presenting problems.

Both Mr. and Mrs. E. were somewhat apprehensive as to what they had to expect in this initial meeting, since neither had ever sought professional help in the past. However, with the basic introductions out of the way and with direct and warm support on the therapist's behalf, they were able to relax sufficiently to describe in detail their attendant problems.

In order to give the reader a proper format for the interviews that follow, I shall briefly outline the specific things which I hope to accomplish in such an initial contact with a patient or patients.

A. I first identify myself, attempt to answer any questions directed to me, and make known that, since I am a therapist and the patient is experiencing difficulties (as in this case), there is a professional reason for our meeting together.

B. I attempt to obtain basic facts by direct questions, providing the patient is not too apprehensive or agitated. This includes how the patient views his problems.

C. I make it clear to the patient that there are no restrictions on use or choice of words or expressions of feelings, providing such expressions of feelings are not harmful to patient or therapist.

D. I usually do not attempt to offer interpretations in the

initial session unless feelings and reactions are of such distortion and of such proportion that an interpretation might assist the patient to view the problem in a more realistic way.

E. I conclude the initial interview by outlining my plan for therapy, presenting the patient with a generalized schedule of meetings, setting fees for services, and discussing finances if this is indicated. The need for mutual cooperation is stressed in terms of maintaining regular continuity of therapy sessions if positive results are to be achieved. I hold out no carrots or magic wand. I feel that this is extremely important for the patient to understand and accept.

THE SECOND INTERVIEW: WITH MRS. E.

Th: Hello, Mrs. E. How do you feel today?

Pt: Mr. M. Do you think that you can help my husband and and me? I know that I love him, but I'm not quite sure how he feels about me.

Th: What do you think makes you say that?

Pt: (Pause) I'm not sure. How can I ever be sure if Al never wants to talk to me? It seems that I'm the one who has the problems. He's so arbitrary, he's the boss, he makes all of the decisions. At times I feel completely wrong and yet I know that I'm right—at least, I think I am. (Long Pause) I guess I'm frightened. (Long Pause).

Th: Frightened?

Pt: Yes, frightened. I keep thinking that Al and I will go our separate ways and then once again I'm a failure.

Th: (Pause) Do you see yourself as a failure because of your first marriage?

Pt: Yes.

Th: Would you like to tell me about it? (Pause).

Pt: (She then describes her first husband, how he drank, his cruelties and emotional outbursts and his refusal to have children. This return to her past was accompanied by a varied display of emotional reactions: crying and fidgeting in her chair.)

Th: Do you really feel that you can compare Al with your former husband?

Pt: (Pause) No, not really. I guess not. That's what attracted me to Al. You see he was my patient, and he was always so kind and considerate, not only of me, but of the other nurses and orderlies who came into his room. Well, he was so different, and I never was used to being treated like I was a person with feelings. (She then went into detail of their courtship and how kind and gentle Al was with her. She talked of their sexual involvement, how she was the aggressor rather than Al, and how afterwards she felt guilty—not because of the sex, but because she felt that perhaps she trapped Al into marrying her.)

Th: Perhaps you feel like this because of your present inability to communicate your feelings to Al.

Pt: Perhaps so, but he always seems so withdrawn, I really feel trapped. I just break down and cry. I know that he resents me when I do this, but I can't help it. (It was here that Mrs. E. first indicated that she was the one who initiated the idea of counseling and her husband's rejection of such help.)

Th: Do you feel that your husband doesn't see any real problems in the marriage?

Pt: I really can't say for sure. I believe that he realizes that we have problems, but I also feel that he perhaps thinks it's all me.

Th: Are you saying that he doesn't see his contribution or involvements in his relations with you as a factor?

Pt: I guess so.

Th: Can you as a person see where possibly you are creating some of the present disturbances?

Pt: (Pause) Well, I'm not sure. Perhaps, I'm afraid that I can't live up to what he expects of a wife.

Th: What does he expect?

Pt: I don't really know. I do know that he's bitter toward women on account of his former wife. She deserted him and took his three children with her. He doesn't like to talk about it, but from what I know, he came home from work one day and found the house deserted. You had better ask him. He might be more open with you.

Th: I intend to discuss this with your husband. One thing you both must learn to realize is that I can help you only as far as each of you want me to. It means that we must learn to trust one another and each of you must feel free to discuss feelings openly. What may seem unimportant to you might be one of the keys we're searching for. Building bridges to closer communication will enable each of you to see each other's feelings and needs in a more realistic and objective way. It will help each of you to gain a deeper understanding of one another. Once this happens, changes in your relationships will gradually emerge.

Pt: I feel that you're right. Anyway, I do feel better just knowing that we're doing something.

(End Of Session)

THE THIRD INTERVIEW: WITH MR. E.

(Mr. E. came to my office accompanied by his wife who waited in the waiting room. Both were chatting amiably together.)

Pt: I noticed your sign on the door says psychotherapist. Could you tell me what psychotherapy is and will you do it with us? How does it work?

Th: I'll be happy to explain this to you. It's not as complicated as it may seem. (I then proceeded to explain in some detail what psychotherapy was and how it could be related to their problems since these problems were generating some inner emotional response.)

Pt: You say that such therapy will help us to untangle our feelings and relate better to one another. Am I right?

Th: Yes, in some respects you are right. However, movement up or down will depend on how you and your wife are able to respond to the guidance and direction which you will receive from our sessions. If you are able to remain free and open in your approaches to the problems within the marriage, gradual insights will be developed, enabling each of you to become more aware of each other's personal needs. You must attempt to realize that many problems within marriage emerge solely because either one or both of the marital partners either tend to attempt to live isolated from one another or go to the other extreme of attempting to change their spouse into what they, as a person, feel a husband or wife should be. Neither of these approaches to marriage can work successfully. Marriage should not deprive a person of his individuality; rather it should enable a man and woman to join forces for the greater good and wholeness of both as a unit, but to still keep the individual nature of each intact. I hope that counseling and psychotherapy will do just this for you and your wife. I also realize that you will become angry at times and be in disagreement with what I say. I want you to feel free to express your feelings in the way most comfortable to you. Do you feel that you understand?

Pt: Yes, but I must admit that I have a lot of questions in my mind, but when I'm here I can't seem to recall things.

Th: This is understandable. But, why not try to jot down things between visits that you perhaps want to talk about. In this way some of your questions as well as your anxieties can be dealt with, so that you will feel more comfortable.

Pt: That seems like a good idea, now, but later on I feel really foolish. Tell me, just how would you describe me?

Th: It's interesting that you should ask me this, since I'm quite interested in how you see yourself, not only as a person but in your relationship with your wife.

Pt: Not as very much I'm afraid. You see, I'm still trying to figure out why my first wife left me. We never had any serious disagreements; well, at least, not what I would call serious. I really thought that we had a good marriage until I came home and found her gone without any word of explanation. I can't tell you how I felt or, for that matter, how I feel. In fact I'm still in the dark.

Th: Perhaps I can help you to clear up some of the feelings which you have regarding your former wife. It would appear that with some of the feelings being generated within your present marriage, the same or similar factors contributed to the breakdown of your former marriage. In other words, whether you realize it or not, your behavior and attitudes were a contributing factor in the decision made by your first wife to leave you.

(A Long Pause)

Pt: (Somewhat Angry) I don't need you to tell me that I drove her away. God knows that I tried to be a good husband and father. If she was so miserable, why didn't she tell me? (Pause).

Th: Perhaps she tried to communicate her feelings to you in ways other than by talking. I really don't know, but, perhaps as we progress in therapy, reasons for past events might become clearer to you.

Pt: Maybe you're right. (Pause) Well, I know you're right in what you say; if you weren't, I wouldn't be having problems in this marriage.

Th: I think it's good for you to begin to come out of yourself, but try to remember that marriage is a continual interaction of two people and the breakdowns within marriage are the results of both people malfunctioning, not just one. So, try not to be too hard on yourself.

Pt: Just one thing more before I go. (Pause) Will you tell me what to do to make this marriage come out OK?

Th: Well, not in so many words. A lot will depend on the situations between you and your wife and how things develop during the course of therapy. Certainly, I'll provide guidance to each of you and, when the occasion warrants it, I'll present alternative courses of action. However, my main role will be to help both you and your wife to gain insight into yourselves as individuals, thereby enabling each of you to view each other more objectively, so that each of you can reach a level of maturity where your individual choices and decisions will achieve some measure of happiness and compatibility rather than dissension and grief.

(There was a brief discussion and the session was terminated)

Reflecting on these first three interviews, the reader can fairly well visualize the interactions between patient and therapist and the various psychotherapeutic approaches which were utilized. Fortunately, in this case illustration, we have a young married couple who are well-educated, as well as highly intelligent. They came to therapy with some awareness that problems existed and, from the onset, recognized the need for professional assistance. With these factors present, it was fairly safe to predict a favorable prognosis for this marriage on an overall level.

In succeeding interviews with both patients, they were able to develop personal insights into their own individual selves and gradually become aware of how they were reacting to each other under specific conditions which faced them in day to day living. Mrs. E. originally presented fearfulness of her husband's reactions and had previously attempted to relate to him as she felt that he would want. Such an approach put her on the defensive, and when positive responses from her husband were not forthcoming, she experienced feelings of rejection and at times much hostility which she attempted to cover. By the same token, Mr. E. rejected his wife's advances for fear of letting down his defenses and possibly placing himself in a vunerable position, something he was determined not to do.

The therapist assumed an active role and helped each person to view his individual self as he existed in the eyes of the other. The gradual self-awareness that emerged enabled each to feel more secure within himself and herself as a person in their normal interaction with one another. Physical, emotional, and verbal responses increased, facilitating communication at all levels. With these new feelings of inner security permeating their relationship, both Mr. and Mrs. E. were gradually able to enter into and resolve problems which here-to-fore they tended to repress or, at best, handle on a superficial level.

As therapy progressed, new problems were uncovered, and it's interesting to see how these were dealt with. The three children of Mr. E.'s first marriage became a real threat to Mrs. E. for she realized that, sooner or later, she would find herself in a person-to-person encounter. The normal concerns of a step-parent were further enhanced by her own feelings of being in competition with Mr. E.'s first wife. In effect, she felt that, no matter what she did in her relations with the children, some degree of criticism would be forthcoming. The first such encounter was during the children's summer vacation when they came to visit their father and step-mother for a period of two weeks.

The following interview brings out some of Mrs. E.'s feelings with reference to this initial visit in August.

THE NINETEENTH INTERVIEW

Mrs. E. came to the office looking fresh and cool in spite of the hot humid weather which we were experiencing. She seemed relaxed and greeted me in a friendly way.

Pt: I have a lot to talk about. Al's children are with us and while it's not as bad as I first thought it would be, I'll be glad when the next week is over and they return home. I seem to be getting along with them famously and we seem to have fun together, until their father walks in. Then, I'm totally ignored and they do exactly what they feel like doing whether I approve or not. (She then went on to describe an incident in which she laid out the children's clothes for church. They refused to wear what she had selected. Rather, they went to their father and had him select the clothes. Mrs. E. reacted to this by telling them to wear what she had put out for them, expecting to have her husband's backing. The outcome was that Mr. E. sided with the children, saying his wife was making a big fuss about nothing. While describing this incident Mrs. E. became quite emotional and alternated between a display of anger and crying. Then she stated quite simply, "I'm telling you all of this because you had advised me of possibly having incidents similar to this and because you seem to understand. I certainly wish Al had some of the same understanding for my feelings.")

Th: I'm sure this must have been difficult for you. But since you yourself recognize that we had previously talked of such possible reactions on behalf of the children, as well as of your husband, why do you permit your feelings to get so out of control?

Pt: I don't know. Somehow I've been trying so hard to make it a pleasant time for the kids as well as for both Al and myself; then I seem to wind up with a kick in the rear end.

Th: You're human.

Pt: At times I don't feel like it.

Th: How do you feel?
    (Long Pause)

Pt: Tired of competing for Al's affection and tired of trying to break through to him.

Th: But, a few weeks ago, you agreed that there have been a lot of breakthroughs and changes. In fact, you even recognized that you are changing in many ways.

Pt: I know, but it all seems so futile at times. I guess I'm a bit upset. All I want is for Al to see me as a person, my feelings, my needs as his wife. I also want to give him children, but I guess that will never happen. He loves children and I'd feel better if we had a child, but I just can't seem to get pregnant.

Th: Do you see children as a bargaining point for Al's affection? Is this why you want a baby?
    (Pause)

Pt: No, not for that. I guess I feel cheated in my first marriage. I really don't feel that a woman is complete unless she's had a baby.

Th: I think I understand.
    (Patient began to cry. Pause of about five minutes.)

Th: Perhaps in our next meeting we can talk about this, since it seems quite important to you. There are ways to work this through and I'll help you.

Pt: I'd like to talk more about it, but I know we can't now, since my time is almost up.

Th: Well, I feel that we should attempt to work one thing through at a time. You will still have the children for another week and perhaps things might start going better now that the ice between you is broken. I think that you should try to realize that strangeness and some apprehension exists on the children's behalf and on your husband's behalf as well as your own. One such meeting will break the ice, but it will take more get-togethers in the future for all of you to feel comfortable and really build up close personal interactions and relations.

I'd advise you to talk over your feelings freely with Al and perhaps you might even agree to accompany him to his conference with me, so that the three of us could have the opportunity to talk over the feelings which you both are experiencing at the present time.

Pt: I'll try to follow through on what you advise, and I'd really like to talk out my feelings with you and Al, if Al doesn't mind my coming with him. I'll certainly speak to him about it. You know, I always feel better after our conferences, and I know that I can work this out. Both Al and you will be proud of me.

(End Of Session)

As therapy continued, both Al and his wife brought out how their relationships were growing and developing with Al's children. In fact, Carol met Al's former wife on several occasions and, while no deep relationships were established, the former Mrs. E. began to accept Carol's sincere interest in the children and no longer attempted to put barriers in the way of the developing relationships between the children and Carol.

Gradually, this couple has developed insight into each other's needs and currently they are successfully working out existing problems. Therapy has been reduced to every three months at a maintenance level. As previously stated, adoption plans are completed, since it has been medically determined that Carol is unable to have children.

In this case presentation, all modes of counseling were utilized from time to time. As a therapist, I have always adopted a strong role, whether it be supportive or active counseling. It's my firm belief that we cannot permit patients or clients to flounder in the morass of their own inadequacies and the confusion resulting thereof. The therapist has a prime responsibility to guide, direct, and channel the thinking and energies of the patient into avenues which will lead to the goals and aspirations which he has set for himself.

In connection with this, I would like to present some basic criteria which, in my opinion, a therapist, counselor, or any practitioner working with patient or client problems should follow. I cannot accept the premise of some of my fellow practitioners who attempt to do therapy by the book. A therapist should be a vital, dynamic being throughout the entire therapeutic process. He should be able to participate with the patient, as well as play the role of observer, depending on the overall therapeutic field and the interaction which may or may not be generated. He should be able to adequately deal with shifting areas of focus, even though there might be little advance evidence of the shifts about to take place. Certainly, a therapist should also be skilled in the art of nonverbal communication in terms of the individual nature which his client or patient presents during the course of therapy. No therapist should ever attempt to mold a patient in his or her concept of what a patient should be, do, or react to. The individual should be encouraged to develop within his own framework of reference and in a manner comfortable to himself.

From time to time, the therapist should evaluate his own responses and reactions to the patient. He should be able to feel comfortable within a therapeutic situation, wherein both dependency and independence are alternately experienced, so that independence can be gradually fostered and, with proper guidelines, therapy can be gradually reduced and eventually terminated, as the patient accepts more and more responsibility for his own actions as a person.

Collaboration with other professionals should be a prime commandment of every therapist. It's very easy, in practicing on one's own, to fall into complacency and to permit individual personal needs to color our approach to the patients' problems. In reexamining our own motivations and gaining objective approaches from our colleagues, both the therapist and the patient will benefit.

INDEX